a view from the

Front Porch

encounters with
life and Jesus

a view from the

Front Porch

encounters with
life and Jesus

Craig D. Lounsbrough

A VIEW FROM THE FRONT PORCH:
ENCOUNTERS WITH LIFE AND JESUS

Published by Revival Nation Publishing

ISBN 978-1-926625-27-0

Printed in the United States of America

Revival Nation Publishing
Ontario • CANADA

P.O. Box 30001
RPO Eastland Plaza
Sarnia, Ontario
N7T 0A7

www.RevivalNationPublishing.com

Foreword

Often I wander through the meandering back roads of my mind. The paths are peaceful, softly winding to gentle places. I discover memories iced with a bit of the frosting of idealism, but real nonetheless.

The memories are laced sweet by spring's blossoms and speckled gold by the sea of dandelions that ebbed across the yard. Frosty root beer floats on heavy, tepid nights. Raucous hours splashing in the pool under lazy, drifting summer skies. The haunting call of geese plying brisk fall skies, lulling the final reds and golds of fall to a deep, seasonal slumber. Crackling fires on bitter winter nights, confidently holding the cold at bay. Dad's never-ending knack for fixing everything, our hearts and our hurts included. Mom's timely arrival with thick, steamy hot chocolate on cold winter days or brisk iced tea to cut summer's humidity. Fishing and frolicking. Trees and toads. Bikes and BB guns. Paper routes and pliable hearts.

These memories form a deep sanctuary, a point of restorative refuge in a world often deluged with destruction and pervaded with pain. But to ascribe them as memories only is to rob and pillage them, to strip them of their treasures. They represent the raw fabric and essence of life fully playing itself out in the freedom of innocence that was yet to be lost. They were young eyes capturing life and freezing it into our memories before those eyes clouded with the pessimism of adulthood. Our hearts were unacquainted with the savage recoil of life. They were widely open to every experience and drinking deep of each moment, committing it to memory for ready retrieval in darker days. All are strands of memory that, when carefully woven through the tapestry of our lives, provide us illuminating meaning, profound understanding, and soothing comfort. The deep well of the past is being drawn into the landscape of the present during times of drought.

I realize that the memories of many are none of the sort described in this book. That is part of my purpose in writing it. I want to both provide the reader with the ability to access the riches of their past and allow those without a past to borrow mine. Hopefully, I have succeeded on both fronts.

The title of the book arises from the place where I often recall these memories: the front porch. Here a number of them were made. And here, many decades later, they are recalled. The front porch represents opposite ends of my life, where many of these memories were fashioned in freedom and innocence, and where they are recalled in a world largely without that freedom and innocence. Many an early morning and late evening are spent on the front porch awash in memory. Memory is the plumb line dropped in the deep well of recollection, drawing its fresh waters into the parched terrain of my present. May God use this book to afford you the same experience.

Contents

Craig D. Lounsbrough

Chapter 1

I Love You

At three, the excitement of Christmas drains little bodies that happily expend themselves in the wide-eyed savoring of tinsel, glass bulbs, twinkling lights and brightly wrapped packages. She was completely exhausted from her daylong embrace of the holiday when I carried my three-year-old daughter to bed late on Christmas Eve. Her arms and legs hung limp, having felt and touched and ran through the wonder of the season until they could feel and touch and run no more. I ascended the stairs and gently pushed open the door of her darkened room. I placed her within the thick folds of the awaiting blankets, and her heavy eyes opened ever so slightly. With eyes laced with the faraway haze and mist of exhaustion, she looked into my eyes and said the four words that no gift awaiting me under the tree could possibly say as well. Softly she mumbled, "I love you, Daddy." A tiny smile curled across her sleepy lips. Then she rolled over and drifted off to sleep.

I descended the stairs, but they looked different. Settling into my chair, I stared deep into the tree. The lights sparkled with a meaning I'd previously missed. Somehow, the holiday was no longer commercial. The intent became distinctly clearer. All the trappings were attempting to embrace one single message: I love you. It was compelling, but it somehow felt vulnerable. Was it that innocent and that simple?

As I eased into the embrace of my chair, the message dissipated all too quickly, becoming lost in the spinning vortex of reality that Christmas intersects once a year. I was inundated by pain, both in my life and in the lives of those around me. Christmas and the assorted trappings seemed an effort to grasp at some fragments of what should be in life but what is not. The story of love seemed to rise out of a longing for something innately deeper, its themes repeated because of its absence in real life. Somehow, if we recited the story and the theme of love associated with it with enough frequency, we could at least believe we were capable of articulating love. If we could articulate it, it was not entirely lost to us, even though we had failed miserably in achieving it. And if we could hold onto even some precariously thin thread of it, maybe there was hope – just maybe.

While I desperately wanted to believe that the words of my daughter had within them the original shards of something astoundingly divine that would stand superior to the horrendous realities of life, my mind told me otherwise. That love, even from the lips of an innocent three-year-old, were, in the end, meaningful but largely powerless. Life was too awful, and love seemed too idealistic, rendering it the stuff of fairytales, teary-eyed idealists, and naive religious fanatics too fearful of theological deficiencies to set Scripture squarely against life.

Sitting there, the jaded nature overcame me as a thick fog that slowly suffocated my daughter's words, their power quickly disseminating. Was my realism justified? Is love nothing more than what we would like, being the stuff of idealistic projection that we can never achieve? How does love as exhibited by God on that night so many years ago stand up against everything that would appear able to crush it with the greatest of ease.

As a pastor and a therapist, I have seen pain in others, whether that be the horrific violation of sexual abuse; the trauma of the sudden abandonment by a spouse; terminal illnesses that instantly redraws the line of death from somewhere out on the horizon of our lives, suddenly scrawling it's blackness directly at our feet; or the inexplicable death of a child that begs for some thin thread of explanation that never comes, that never fills the scathing hole left in a parent's heart in order to give reason to tragedy.

My own pain, on innumerable fronts, has frequently left me a crippled mass of emotional flesh, engulfed in agonies that cruelly defy words that might somehow capture my pain and give it an identity. If the words were given, they might provide me recourse against the pain. But words are all too often absent. In the swill of it all, I must carry the crippling weight of my own agony while simultaneously helping others survive theirs. I must go to bed at night having no idea how I survived the day. How does love stand in the face of these horrors and a million others like them? *I am jaded,* I thought as I stared into the twinkling lights – and for good reason. My mind drifted …

Love Comes

It was 60 long miles of unrelenting contractions, birth being held at bay. There was deep confusion in her mind, dropping a plumb line of disorienting doubt into her soul. The Son of God born like this? Under these circumstances? The chaos of events, of timing and of circumstance hardly set the stage that one would visualize for a coming king. None of them remotely reflected the birth Mary had conceptualized for the previous nine months. Everything seemed to be at terrible odds with the message of the angel and how she had imagined it all happening. Why the census now? Why the census at all?

There is the plan of God, and then there is how we perceive that plan. The two are often strikingly different, at times incongruent, beyond the scope of human logic, leaving all the might of our mental processes incapable of achieving even the remotest shred of reconciliation. The resultant residue of doubt then wreaks spiritual debilitation. And for Mary, they were terribly at odds, creating an emotional angst that matched the unrelenting contractions that pressed ever harder. The donkey took a misstep; Mary was jostled; and the contractions surged again. As had happened throughout the long arduous day, the barren landscape vanished once more in the tidal surge of blurring pain. The thoughts of a teenage Jewish girl were obscured by agony and equally smeared by uncertainty.

It sat on a limestone ridge framed by two summits that seemed to have drawn themselves up from the plains. A saddle-like hollow between them gently cradled the city of Bethlehem. The city was set in an amphitheater of hills as if anticipating a grand drama, a drama set to unfold on a stage of obscurity. The climb was a demanding one, rising 2,500 feet. The ascent was laborious, layering exhaustion upon exhaustion.

The arrival was marked by yet another ascent: that of navigating the jostling crowds. Vendors called out in boisterous tones, hawking their wares amidst droves of sweaty pack animals. Shuffling, startled, lowing, fighting attending reins, they reluctantly coursed through tight streets into the ever-deepening throng, caught in the suction of the masses. Pigeons burst from lofty precipices in a flush of frantic feathers: circling, regrouping, and then landing high above the bustle on precarious ledges. Their bobbing heads frantically attempted to discern any potential threats that might arise out of the predatory landscape that milled about below them. They were tentative. Squads of armored centurions walked in lockstep formation, the thick metallic rattle of swords and sabers accentuating each step. Cavernous alleys stood rock tight, refusing to acquiesce to the crowds who pressed against their cold limestone walls as they navigated into the bowels of the city. It was mayhem.

Somewhere in the sea of pressing humanity, a busy innkeeper paused long enough to offer some shelter. It was nothing more than a cave, but it was nothing less. It was crudely carved out of the lifeless limestone ridge that generally sat below the place of residence. Mary and Joseph stared at each other. Exhaustion had washed their faces with furrowed lines and set eyes deep in darkened sockets. At least the stable had been cleaned. Feed and hay had been put up in preparation for the census. The animals were bedded for the night, providing some slight measure of privacy. It was theirs if they wanted it. In the midst of their exhaustion, they agreed because exhaustion seeks reprieve regardless of the manner in which it's obtained.

The door creaked open. The couple was immediately met by the sharp smell of fresh urine. Musty odors – a dense mixture of manure, straw, feed, and the thick coats of stable animals – wafted thick through the damp air. The bleating of sheep was absorbed in soft piles of fodder. The unsettled jostling of cattle in their stalls gave depth to the greeting darkness. Donkeys shifted tentatively, the soft thud of their hooves suggesting silent anticipation.

Mice scurried along walls into dark corners, vanishing in deep mounds of fresh hay. An owl greeted the night, the call distant and haunting. The barking of a dog floated in tentatively from the darkness of a world finding itself sleepy. The muffled voices of a world settling for the night drifted down vacant streets in scant and ever blurry tones. A dim light from a flickering lamp cast a vague and tentative glow across a yawning stable; it's soft, dancing light exposing the scene, but silently so.

Joseph eye's darted around the stable. Thoughts racing quickly, he created a place in the fresh hay. Soon the piercing cries of a young woman cut deep into the thick limestone and were then absorbed into the attending mounds of hay. Animals were startled, then settled. The light remained steady and unabated as would the light of this Savior. Sweat traced glistening lines down a strained face, collecting and then dripping off her chin. Her hair was drenched in soaked strands that flattened themselves against a face wracked with pain. Her features were mottled in deep red, etched with the pain of birthing a Savior.

Joseph himself, tentative and concerned, scurried about in confusion, wanting to take upon himself some of the immensity of the pain. However, he was forced into solitude, as was Mary. He was helpless only to watch, to be in company with the rest of creation as, for a moment, all that existed held its breath. History and eternity were about to shift, to pivot on this single moment. The light flickered, bathing the scene in soft golds, waltzing with tentative shadows that could only admire the light from a distance – unless they were consumed by it. The animals settled into a near reverence. Darkness made way for a myriad scattering of stars to join, ushering in a waiting cosmos. Something of majesty had been lavished across the stable, rendering it holy.

The night was not disappointed. Finally, the cry of a newborn replaced the cries of His mother. It was new but strong. Breathing into His lungs the musty air around Him, God felt a body He'd created, from the inside out. It was strange and unfamiliar. Instinctively, Mary removed the mucus from His mouth and nose. His soft, pink body, trembling at the violent transition from heaven's perfection to earth's alien imperfection, was wiped clean of blood and amniotic fluid. The All-powerful was now completely helpless. Eternal independence was completely dependent upon a trembling teenage girl, exhausted and soaked in sweat.

Mary bared a breast and raised the infant to her. He settled and calmed, easing into the turbulent transition from one world to a very different one. Tiny fingers that shaped mountains and threw galaxies into deep space wrapped themselves around Mary's finger. Trembling legs grew calm in the radiant warmth of the swaddling clothes that gently engulfed Him. God was here – finally. Thousands of years of prophecies were completed. The hope and desire of so many who expectantly scanned the horizons of the future were fulfilled. A single expectation that gave millions the ability to face their times and their eras with hope was now a reality.

Creation exhaled. Angels shouted. A rousing cheer shook the halls of heaven in wild applause. The invasion had commenced. God smiled, knowing that the event promised from eternity past was completed. It was finished.

Viable, Believable Love
A manger that day would be followed by a cross another. An entrance was made at the lowest place in humanity, with an exit looming at an even lower one. The words "It is finished" were to be heard again, only differently. Both events were emblazoned in love. Perfect love would come face to face in a raw, primordial clash with the manifest horrors of sin. It would have to stand, and it did. Its power was not the issue, although it appeared to be. The issue was the shallowness of man – my shallowness – to grasp the depth of love. It is our unspoken assumption that, set squarely on the thin veneer of human logic, love will eliminate pain, wiping it from the landscape of our lives by its sheer power. It is a rationale quite appropriate for the limitations of human love, but it is sorely inadequate when understanding God's love. The presumed nature of love is to desire the freedom, or more appropriately, the liberation, of that which is loved. Love is about rescue, for anything less would be cruel and hardly loving – or so we believe.

But love is infinitely more powerful and more profound than simply its ability to eradicate pain – far more powerful. God designed love to be massive enough to live in pain and subdue pain's attributes for phenomenal growth. In a desperate but profound moment, Jesus said, My prayer is not that you take them out of the world ... (John 17:15 NIV), as God's love was designed to be inserted into the world's pain to work pain against itself for our good. James seized the idea when he wrote, Consider it pure joy, my brothers, whenever you face trials of many kinds, because you know that the testing of your faith develops perseverance. Perseverance must finish its work so that you may be mature and complete, not lacking anything (James 1:2-4 NIV).

Loves does not live with the insecurities that demand it eliminate pain in order to insure its own survival. It is able to handily overpower pain and use pain's energy against pain's intent, seizing its power and bending it to our growth so we lack nothing. Love has the power to change the force, direction and the nature of pain so we gain so very much more than simply its elimination. Pain is for our profit in God's pursuit of our perfection. We gain its power turned in our favor, reaping growth unimagined, rather than having squandered the power of pain by its removal. ... we also rejoice in our sufferings, because we know that suffering produces perseverance; perseverance, character; and character, hope (Romans 5:3-4 NIV). Rich is pain in the hands of love.

God's plan did not involve the eradication of pain for the waste that such an action would incur. Instead, love involved inserting Himself as perfect love into the middle of all mankind's sordid pain. The newborn cry that proclaimed the implementation of that plan rose that night from an isolated manger set deep in mankind's pain. And from that place, Jesus would walk the back roads of mankind's pain right up to a barren hill set with three crosses. He did not eradicate pain. He subdued it and forged it into a tool that would forge us into His image. Love is not lenient; it is lethal in shaping us into His likeness.

The manger settled. Animals calmed and drifted off to sleep. Mary and Joseph felt the effects of the events, and they settled into the consuming fatigue. Calm gently enshrouded the barn as God pulled up a blanket of stars and tucked in the horizon. Unbeknownst to those in the manger, the applause of heaven had burst the seams of heaven itself, spilling a cavalcade of angels to shepherds in fields nearby. They would soon visit and welcome the King. They were the honored first of billions to be touched by this birth.

The city drifted off to sleep. Business would resume the next day. The census would continue. Bartering, bantering and trading would be transacted in the open air markets that lined streets now steeped in darkness. Meals would be cooked. Marriages performed. Clothing mended. Children would romp in dusty streets. Rome would rule. Birth and death would roll on in the unfolding human drama. Eternity had been shaken, but earth felt not a ripple. God had come, disguised, quietly and unobtrusively, slipping into human history and human pain. The Creator entered His creation on tiptoe, saying in the most profound way, I love you.

Back Home
A hand on my shoulder drew me back to the tree. Then I saw my wife's gentle smile. The lights twinkled in pinpoints of excitement. My daughter's words settled into my head, warm and inviting recollection over and over, and finally I got it. I realized her words were not designed to eliminate my pain nor the horrors of life around me. Pain and love are not the either/or of life, being somehow mutually exclusive. Opposite though they may be, it is the energy of the friction between them that, when harnessed, molds us into Christ-likeness. Life's assorted horrors bespeak of opportunities that love desires to seize in building this Christ-likeness into our lives. Her love took my pain and turned it against itself, harnessing its power to be unleashed in my life in order to bring remarkable growth. Suddenly it made sense. Love does not eradicate pain; it turns it back on itself for my good. Pain then is growth waiting to happen. It is the ingredient God uses to bring Christ-likeness to my life.

How immense to be loved by God with the same love that drove Him to slice open the expanse of the eternal in order to step into the carnage and filth of this place. How much more unimaginable to realize not simply that He came, but what He came to do. The lights seemed brighter, the season immeasurably fuller. The words I love you emanated from the heart of a daughter and the heart of God Himself. My heart was full with the applause of heaven resonating in my soul. Life was given new meaning in light of the pain around me. I savored the words "I love you" as that night demanded they be savored. It was truly a wonderful time of the year.

Pondering Point
The concept of love is poorly conceived and terribly marginal. It is incomprehensibly contrary to the voice of our culture that espouses love based on pay-offs, conditional returns, and the promised eradication of pain. That is not love at all, but a modality of trading affection for the acquisition of some desired asset with no intent for growth. But we have embraced such transactions and definitions as love, thereby forfeiting, by our own ignorance, the power and irrepressible magnitude of love that causes all things [to] work together for good (Romans 8:28 KJV). Love was unleashed in a Bethlehem manger. God forfeited godhood to save us from the tragedy and travesty of perfection having gone terribly astray. He abandoned all that was rightfully His in the endeavor. Yet, He had every right to walk away from a creation that had walked away from Him. God

became man and in the becoming, still allowed man to reject His offer of salvation and redemption. That is truly love without conditions. Such actions ooze with the stuff of authentic affection.

A Thought

- Do I hold to cheap love that promises the escape from pain, a promise that it can't deliver?
- Am I willing to submit myself to a love that will not save me from pain, but will fully support me in that pain in order that I might grow into Christ-likeness?
- If not, am I willing to live a marginalized life that will miss all God has?

Chapter 2

A Leather Belt and a Three Dollar Buckle

Gangly and pimple faced, he stood pensively on the arriving cusp of adolescence. He stared down the long corridor of his life; the path wound from uncertainty to uncertainty. His movements were cumbersome and terribly awkward, having been set to the chaotic cadence of abuse. Stumbling and uncoordinated, he tripped across a life script measured out and metered in notes of deep pain. He had long, pencil thin limbs that, despite enduring effort, found little ability to flow and function in unison. Deftly uncoordinated, he bumbled through life. Wiry glasses were set across a thin face of confusion, pain and fear. Worn polyester pants and thin cotton shirts were the stuff of thrift stores and secondhand shops. His was indeed a secondhand life.

He pensively reached out to the world around him. He desperately tried to be right and do right in order to have that world nod in agreement at some success, despite how minor. Each effort was slapped with the thick rod of ridicule and beaten with words dipped deep in the slurry of caustic criticism. Inevitably, he would crawl away into dark corners of his bedroom – and his life, where he drew up into deep shadows, wincing and crying. Knowing no solace except isolation, his heart and his body were strewn with senseless lacerations. He was alone – desperately so.

Jonathon was barely 12 years of age and already an outcast. He was relegated out beyond the fringes of society by parents who birthed him, then rejected him. They beat a helpless baby and abused an infant whose tiny eyes were filled with the desire for acceptance in the midst of rejection. His parents, seized and satiated with incomprehensible evil, extinguished cigarettes on his tender skin and snuffed out hope in his heart. They dropped him on his head for personal amusement and levity. Repeatedly, they had forced him naked into the backyard with welts swelling across his back from the sharp snap of his father's thick leather belt: evidence of relentless beatings for trifling mistakes, sometimes for no mistakes at all. Many nights he was left outside to sleep with the dog while the rest of world stayed inside.

Sexual abuse would follow, rendering him a helpless party to the most putrid of human actions, culminating in the violation of a life too small to protect itself, much less comprehend any need to do so. His was a life too tender and innocent to understand the abuse perpetrated upon it. He found himself peering back, his face pressed again the glass from outside the world, longing to belong. He longed to have the world invite him back in and for it to create a place where he knew he mattered and had value, a place where he counted for something.

Jonathon was a reject in likely the most complete form I had ever encountered. He was a discarded piece of emotionally maimed humanity wrapped in a 12-year-old body. His pain had deeply marinated throughout a tender 12-year-old soul. His was a life soaked in the blood of a soul martyred for the amusement of troubled parents. A heart mutilated for merriment. A life sacrificed for the sick sexual pleasure of others. A depository of deviance, his life was depleted at 12. And when he was no longer of value to those who had used him, the drama was raised to a crescendo of accumulated cruelty: He was discarded. He was finally abandoned on a desolate road that stretched into a desert of nothingness with little more than cacti, brittle sage, and an endless ribbon of simmering asphalt. Waves of shimmering heat rippled against the arid landscape and sucked the desert dry. He was the same inside. Eventually, he was found wandering and dehydrated by a kind deputy sheriff. And it was there, in the psychiatric hospital, I met the remnant of this little boy, the pieces that were left of whatever he once was, if he ever was anything.

I could only presuppose what Jonathon would have been like had he not lived those 12 years of hell. What could he have been? What would he have been? Latent and deep, under layers of stratified emotional chaos that marked the epochs of his life, there lay a glint of something profound, something precious. It was there, and it was real despite the magnitude of his outbursts, the innumerable moments when the accumulated carnage of his life would erupt to the surface in the molten lava of rage, rendering him a seething vegetable of the abuses of others. Even then, there was something remarkable about him, something flagrantly rich and wonderful that even his most outrageous moment could not hide. There were flecks of diamonds in the midst of his detonations. His was a gifted child, beaten and abused into oblivion. A wonderment grossly misshapen by cruel hands into an oddity. A freak. But it was still there: something precious, gross in its deformity, but there. And I saw it.

Belts and Abuse

Jonathon refused to wear belts. Much of the beatings he had incurred were at the hands of his father, deftly using a thick leather belt. Seasoned and supple by countless beatings, it had been cinched tightly around his hands to hold him while the sexual excesses of others were perpetrated upon him. Drawn tight around his neck, it had coerced obedience from horror. Not a fashion accessory. Rather, it was an instrument of horror and a tool of terror, an implement of undiluted evil.

When his father's belt was confiscated by the authorities, it was found to have traces of blood splattered across its leather surface. Bits of skin were found embedded in its crevices: a testament to brutality. Jonathon would not wear a belt. No wonder. The sight of a belt would traumatize him, rendering him a fleshy infantile pile of trembling humanity that whimpered in the labyrinth of a million horrid memories of abuse. Each screamed at the top of its lungs, callously throwing their sordid pictures vividly across the forefront of a panicked mind. The torrential deluge of years inundated a brutalized heart that had no more defense against the memories than he had when they were originally seared into his brain and branded on his heart. He was held in the clutches of memory that seemed as real as the original moment, rendering Jonathon a prisoner shackled to the horror of his past. I often cried for him. So did others. Sometimes, I still do.

I would never wear my belt around Jonathon. The symbolism was so stringent and overpowering for him that he could not see beyond the belt to the person. His mind halted at the specter. Its symbolism was so deeply entrenched by the welts and blood that its presence was consuming. And so I never wore one – ever.

It Rules Us

What do you want with us? (Luke 4:34 NIV) He heard the words leap out of his mouth, brazen, yet somehow tentative. But they were not his. The experience was surreal. He valiantly struggled against the moment, but he was subdued. The voice was bold, flagrant and narcissistically flamboyant, thin but powerful. Controlling him, the words seemed to slither about the room, striking here and then there, shaking the congregants gathered.

The contemptuous attitude of the enemy was obviously unchanged since he was cast from heaven with his minions. (Satanic evil has no means of redemption because it will not permit itself any and so it remains unchanged.) Raw and fiendish, he delivered a taunt and issued a challenge, unabated evil so taken by the frenzy of its own blackness that it counted itself invincible. Have you come to destroy us? (Luke 4:34 NIV) He blatantly tested the resolve of God and overstated his strength as that of many. A skirmish was set to occur that was but a portent of a cataclysmic battle that stands not far away on the horizon of time.

Then the demon executed a bold maneuver, an attempt to exercise power by naming the adversary. I know who you are – the Holy One of God! (Luke 4:34 NIV) The vying for the power of this life had commenced with an agenda for every life mirrored in this single one. The enemy had infiltrated a soul and infiltrated the very house of God. He had shown his deceptive ability as profound – marvelous even.

Full-blown evil walks among God's people unnoticed. The worst of evil may be invisible evil. I am reminded that evil can insert itself in the very places where I would assume its absence and, therefore, miss its presence. To evil, nothing is sacred. His contempt for God is as commensurate as the raw evil that defines him: evil resident even in belts.

The battle was then engaged. Jesus had seen it before. There had been a great battle in heaven where evil took excessive stock of itself, betrayed God, and was vanquished with the betrayer. Being wrapped in the rage of his own defeat, he was cast to the earth. He now roams that domain with a single intent: the destruction of mankind. If he cannot destroy God, he will destroy that which bears His image. And well he has performed. He was performing there, yet again. A decisive countermove was made by this Nazarene. Be quiet ... come out of him! (Luke 4:35 NIV) The two things that lead to freedom are pronounced: the silencing of that which haunts us and then its removal.

There was a sudden internal wrenching in the man that was not of the man, but the colliding and engaging of two opposing forces fighting for supremacy. Tearing at the man's core, they met in lethal combat on the battlefield of his soul. In the savagery of the spiritual skirmish, he was thrown and helplessly flung to the floor, heaving a thrall of deep panic across the crowded room. The forces vying for his life were infinitely superior to the sum total of his own energies. He was a helpless physical manifestation of a titanic, inward clash where irreconcilable forces sought to occupy the same space and make the same claim. As soon as it had begun, it was over. The battlefield was cleared of the enemy. The diabolical forces that stood arrayed across the landscape of his life were suddenly and inexplicably silent and then absent. All was quiet.

Cognizance stirred within him, tentatively at first and then, with greater force. The caustic fog of possession thinned, drifted and then dissipated. Where am I? In what place had the demonic force left him at that moment? At what place in his life? He was uncertain who he was, much less where he was, his identity having long been lost to an occupying force. That identity was restored by a liberating force. The occupying force having been swept away by the holy and passionate blitzkrieg of God unleashed, the Lord scourged all traces of evil from his life. Freedom was an unfamiliar and alien feeling to him. It demanded that he must initiate; he must decide; he must determine what to do next in the massive void of decisions no longer being dictated by an occupying enemy. And so he lay on the floor, paralyzed by freedom.

His eyes were clear and sharp, becoming tight with discernment. A carpenter's calloused hand, thick and broad, was extended downward to him. The face was firm, but warm; intentional, but relaxed. The silence of irrefutable victory marked His features; the calm of confidence defined Jesus' eyes. Deep in the chiseled face, there bespoke authority, but of a far different kind. It was an authority inexplicably superior to that which had ruled him – so vastly superior that it could ill be defined even in the context of the infinite stretches that it resided in. It was the power of authentic freedom that both begged and invited one onward to wild liberation, the ecstasy of all the assorted shackles and fetters of enslavement having dropped powerless to the floor of one's life. All barriers to restoration and to the making of one complete had been vanquished and had vanished. The authority to restore his assets and his course in life to its original intent had acted. He was himself – himself restored.

What Possesses Me Defines Me

I am a muddled compilation of myriad things that define me. Things lay their claim to my life, exercise control over it, and proclaim, by virtue of these things, who I am. The agreements I have made with these things do indeed allow them to define me. I empower them when I surrender by agreeing that I am what they have defined me to be. There is, on occasion, that voice that shouts, "I am other than this!" There is then a momentary wrestling and contending with what controls me; my own past and the things that illicit that past are much like a leather belt. These things are vastly stronger and I am subdued by them in the wrestling. I eventually surrender to something less than authentic, as a marginalized self is set against the real self and subdues me yet again. And far too often, I have no power to break it, being doomed to not being.

But this possessed man was on the floor before Jesus, and that which possessed him was broken. An alien and unfamiliar sense of authentic self rushed in and flooded the concourses of his life. It filled the corridors and inundated him with himself, with everything that made him uniquely him. It was all terribly unfamiliar but perfectly familiar all at once. He was, in essence, freed to be born again. On the floor, the birth had begun.

The congregants bound by awe, found their voices. The sound of awestruck humanity drew him back to consciousness. This Jesus was now kneeling before him, His eyes intent, both knowing the birth and watching it transpire. This man was being created for the second time. This prophet, this Jesus, drew in the wonder of if all over again.

He is always fascinated by new birth as it is never diminished or dissipated for Jesus. Love creates out of love and because of it. Love can do nothing else. If love is not creating, it is not love. Therefore, it must always be about the business of creating. If love possesses a point of weakness that renders it vulnerable in order that it may be complete, this is it: Jesus loves and here a soul is created yet again.

Scripture records no words exchanged between the two. The speculation of conversation is left to the fog and lost pages of history. But birth needs no explanation. It is the manifest love of God expressing its infinite fullness in a finite package. God defines His infinite characteristics in a human form so terribly limited, but created with limitations yet so vast that God finds ample room to manifest Himself in it; terribly marvelous yet wholly mysterious.

I am no different. I, too, am possessed. Maybe differently, with different things, but it is possession nonetheless. These things claim me; they control me; they strip me of the infinite characteristics of my true self and give me a diminished, dismembered and marred identity at which I am too frequently aghast. Worse yet is to accept this identity in the defeat of self. Indeed it is God who can wrench those things from my life. It is God who can sweep clean the battlefield of my soul and deluge me in the unique characteristics that define the work of the Master in me.

And so, he reached up and clasped the hand of his liberator. The grip was firm. He was about to step into this new life. The power of Jesus' grasp was so sure, so strong, that he was thrust to his feet. Jesus' hand, calloused, thick and broad, rested its weight on his shoulder. The assembled congregants were lost in the emotional catacombs of unbelief, astonishment and euphoric emotional trauma, immobilized by the impossible and stunned by the spectacular. One more look deep into His eyes and the two parted ways. He had met his Maker, and in that meeting, his Maker remade him.

Another Belt
There was a tap on my shoulder. By then I had developed a relationship with Jonathon. So had several others. Trust had been nurtured in the rich loam of consistent love, its seeds having been cradled in the tepid warmth of time spent. Soft waters of gentle affirmation had been tenderly applied to numerous wounds, had soaked through rough husks, and softened parched seeds. Their heads were pressing above the surface and then came a tap on my shoulder.

I turned. It was Jonathon. And in his hand was something most remarkable. In feeble hands, he held a leather belt. But it was much more; it was a leather belt that he had made and shaped and crafted himself. Setting his hands and his heart to the very thing that struck such terror in his heart, it was intricate and ornate, crafted to perfection by hands that were beaten and tied by just such an object. He had stained it to beautiful brown hues. And then, he had added a brass buckle, deeply polished so that light would effortlessly dance with abandon on its nearly glassy surface. It cost me three dollars, he said. On the buckle ... my name: Craig. I'm not afraid anymore, he said. See, I'm not afraid anymore!

The world stopped. All went quiet around me and dissipated into that belt and the gangly 12-year-old who held it out to me. A broad smile of success was drawn from one side of his thin face clear to the other. Relish his victory: He was born again, a second birth. Maybe, for Jonathon, it was his first. I don't know. And then the words that forced me to catch myself as their weight fell: It's for you; I made it for you. I took in my hands the very thing that had imprisoned this marvelous young man and the very thing from which he was now liberated. He had lived their messages. He had been held captive to their assorted horrors. His life had been dictated by them, and now he was free. His thin arms were outstretched with the belt draped across tender hands. He handed me a symbol of the very thing that had held him. We hugged and we cried.

Today, some 23 years later, I still have that belt. I always will. It is a reminder of what held Jonathon and defined his life. But far greater and far grander, it is evidence that we need not be held by that which holds us, that we all can be remade.

Pondering Point
There is something in every life that holds us and defines us, something that so shapes us we come to believe we are that thing, or that event, or that piece or part of our history. Helplessly defined in ways that are other than who and what we really are, we are held captive to a life that is not that for which we were crafted and created. It is no small thing to realize this. And it is a marvelous thing to break from it.

It is about realizing that Jesus frees us from that which we can't liberate ourselves. When we embrace the reality of that which binds us, and we hold fast to the belief that the choice to be freed from it is ours to make, we can strip it of its power, hold it in our hands without fear, and shout to the world, I'm not afraid anymore.

A Thought

- What defines my life and defines me?
- Where do those definitions come from?
- What have I lost in embracing them as defining who I truly am?
- Am I willing to break from them and be who God created me to be?

Chapter 3

Darren and the Plastic Fish

It was a dollar store bin filler, indelibly stamped with "Made in China," that bordered on being junk. There were numerous needs in Darren's life, so numerous that he himself was lost in them. They were pathetic and endless – so it seemed. A plastic fish was little more than a cheap toy that momentarily anesthetized a childlike mind trapped in the deterioration of a 35-year-old body. It was a mere trinket, a point of focus upon which to forget the realities that had bent, and ultimately broken, him. It served as a pathetic distraction from all that had cut thick furrows across his head and heart far too prematurely. It was a cheap, plastic fish.

The years had stooped his shoulders and lined his hair with ever lighter shades of premature gray, cutting deep fissures across his brow and thickening his young skin. His gait had been reduced to a shallow shuffle. He dragged thick shoes across coarse pavement. He wore the soles thin on the outside edges, further canting his gait. His soul was much the same, deeply worn along the outside edges, throwing into a precarious imbalance the cadence of an already distorted life. Darren found himself limping through a world that placed ultimate premiums on that which is new, believing that any value is inherent only in the degree of newness an object possesses. The world viewed his worn edges as old, used up and spent. He was unfairly evaluated as discarded humanity and rendered invisible to the eye of a world too busy.

Baggy pants were thread thin at the knees and frayed at the pockets with stitching pulled and strained at the seams. An oversized shirt bespoke of his desperate efforts to fit into life. Like his shirt, it never happened. Stained and limp, a faded handkerchief hung from a weary pocket. A mouthful of decay filled each smile and poured out in conversation. Chapped lips were edged thick by coarse stubble sprouting from a grimy bed of mottled skin. The expanse of his squared jaw and sunken cheeks were covered with a bumper crop of inattention. His words were primitive and slurred, rolling off his tongue in seamless bursts that made comprehension nearly impossible. Shoulders were drawn down by the weight life had exerted on him, pulling him forward in a Neanderthal sort of cadence that was long and slothful. And he wanted to show me his plastic fish.

"Kind of like the disciples, huh? They caught fish. They were fishermen!" he said. A broad smile showed he anticipated a response from me. Darren was 35, yet he was enamored with a dollar store plastic fish. Like the disciples, huh? His persistence accelerated my desire to talk to a real adult. Church was over, and there were many candidates milling about. My momentary objective was to determine how to terminate this infantile conversation and find someone with some shred of intelligence to whom I could talk. I moved to close the conversation with Darren, and did so quite deftly – I thought. I imagined he would have no idea I had ditched him. As I stepped away from him, he held the plastic fish in his weathered hands as if it were a precious treasure and muttered softly, "I was a sinner; now I'm a fisher of men, too."

God Strikes
There are unexpected moments in life when God sends simplicity as a blinding light that is far more pure and infinitely superior to all the intellectual musings I could devise. Darren's words, "sinner and now fisher of men," though soft, backlit my soul in blinding light and thundered through the very core of my egocentric spirit. They rocked me, simultaneously illuminating my flagrant sense of superiority as paper thin and backlighting my egotistical self against something far greater and far grander. A light both brilliant and revealing was thrown onto something I had unknowingly lost in the dark pool of piousness and shallow Christianity. ("Sinner and fisher of men" are two opposites represented by chilling sin sheathed in death on one end and salvation and humanly unexplainable privilege on the other.) He had seized something spiritually authentic that was indefinably powerful because of its innocent simplicity.

His words drew me down, my soul melting into repentant puddles on the pavement and pooling around Darren's feet. And in my heart, a stark thought shot through my brain. It seized my heart and surged through my soul as the light exposed the grotesqueness of my immaturity. "Go away from me, Lord; I am a sinful man!" (Luke 5:8 NIV). I had rarely felt so abjectly ugly and so starkly far from God. Darren had brilliantly backlit my existence with a handful of simple words, a plastic fish and an innocent life. I was repulsed by what I saw in myself.

Fish and Light
The cool of the night drifted by. Time drifted with it. Waves gently lapped the weathered wooden hull as if the night was completely pacified with simply existing. Sails flapped passively, rolling in a dance with an occasional listless breeze that floated out from somewhere deep in the night. The timbered creaking of shifting weight was soft against the darkness. Oars dipped deep and silently, spinning tiny whirlpools of water that softly gurgled in the thin veil of satin moonlight. The damp scent of water gathered in a thin veneer layer of mist that tentatively skirted the water's surface. The night was intermittently rendered musty with the odors of nets, wet with nothing but water. A distant heron hauntingly called into the night from a far shore. Muffled voices and the lights of other boats drifted listlessly across the water.

Nets were cast, a spinning arch launched by thick arms sure with experience. Slapping the water, they were given a moment to sink. Descending, the keel of the boat became smaller in the submerged descent. The chalky white moonlight was broken into a million, moving shards of milky light on the underside of the waves, fading as the depths were listlessly plumbed. The water cooled, darkened, and was stirred by soft currents. All was listless, a dreamlike descent.

And then – a massive tug; the net reeled and folded in upon itself, instantly enfolding everything within it. A series of firm tugs followed. Lunging toward the surface, it broke the liquid plane and was hauled into the coarse belly of the boat. Again, it was the same, nothing but weeds and water. There was a gruff remark, then a curse edged rough with the abrasion of frustration. Frustration was manifested and expelled into the night by exasperated fishermen whose finest skills could not coerce the deep waters to offer up their bounty should they choose to withhold it. The net was hurriedly prepared and launched again and again and again; the frustrating feeling eternal.

The moon slowly descended to sleep behind the horizon. The stars, adrift across the expanse of the velvet blackness, moved in unison with the universe, the winds of heaven blowing them to the same horizon. Night would soon drift into day. The nets remained empty. Soon the sun stirred with the first tentative band of pastel light on a yawning horizon, softly illuminating empty boats. So went the night.

This was his world, that of his father and his grandfather. His was a lineage of weary boats, hemp nets, flapping fish glinting in flashes of silver, sails and storms. He was isolated within the world of sleeping by day and trolling by night as the fish rose to cooler waters. Lost in this world of his, he was so engrossed in its demands that he was defined by that world, having standardized everything else by its shape and form. This world of nighttime fishing and the life that went with it dictated the shape, tenor and tone of his existence. It was so familiar and natural that becoming it was, for Simon Peter, being who he was and where he needed to be.

There was little thought of anything else, for he knew nothing else. There was no other world other than the methodical frustration of sparse nets, contrary winds, too few fish to market, leaving purses thin with coinage, long nights followed by exhausting days with the only promise being more of the same. Nothing else had backlit his life enough to see anything different.

In His World
But there was an unexpected intrusion, a carpenter turned prophet. Word had spread, rumors of miracles had drifted across the lake, having reached the shoreline and lapped against the wooden hulls of the docked boats. It was likely that many of the fishermen had gotten wind of Him as their sails might have caught a slight breeze. But it was of little importance. Rather, it was an inconvenience. The night had been long and fruitless, the nets yielding nothing more than water, weeds and weariness. There was no fish to market that day. The next night would be pressed with the need to make up for a night lost. It was time for sleep, troubled sleep at best, but sleep nonetheless. But there was an intrusion. Of all days!

The crowd grew, giving some degree of credibility or celebrity status to whoever this was. They picked up a few words here and there, discerning pieces that remained only fragments within the fatigue that enshrouded their minds. Religion wouldn't catch fish and nice words wouldn't mend nets. Sweeping platitudes wouldn't feed hungry families.

But Simon had seen firsthand what was blowing on the winds of rumor. A mother-in-law had been healed. The crippled were walking, pensively but surely, on unfamiliar legs with crutches abandoned at their feet. The crutches were once a necessity, but had been instantly rendered unnecessary. The blind aligned faces with voices for the first time, turning to drink in deep blue skies and finding themselves hopelessly enamored by mounds of brilliant wildflowers. The pallor of death was swept from the faces of catatonic infants, instantly washed alive with vitality that had no explanation, except – he had seen it.

He had attempted to correlate it with his world of boats, frayed nets, canvas sails and fish. It had not changed him. It was an anomaly only because his world had not been directly intersected.

And then, Jesus was in Simon's boat, dead center in Simon's world, ground zero. Boat turned podium and fisherman turned chauffeur. From the bow of this tired fishing vessel, the words of Jesus droned on. It was not that they are not compelling; they simply fell upon a mind dulled with fatigue and deluged with both empty nets and empty pockets. Scripture does not indicate that what Jesus said struck Simon. It was what He did. And then the command came. The nets had already been mended, cleaned and stowed. Weary sails had been drawn tight and tied. Arms were weak and heads were fuzzy. The fish had undoubtedly descended to cooler waters, far beyond the reach of their nets and all of their accumulated skills. And yet, this Jesus wanted to go fishing. The logical argument was of no use; a lifetime of experience was discarded and discounted by this teacher. He was confidently insistent. And so, wearily, Peter mumbled, "But because you say so, I will let down the nets" (Luke 5:5 NIV). And he did.

Oars were lowered by weary fishermen who exchanged glances washed in confusion, anger and a slight flush of stupidity for agreeing to this idiotic venture. Plunged into cool waters, they created spiraling eddies in their wake. The morning sun was full, having long lifted itself off the horizon of a new day, spilling a cascade of gold that broke into sparkling flecks of yellow glitter on gentle waves. Oars were drawn in with glistening droplets falling from their weathered edges, ever so quickly catching a slight fleck of sunlight before becoming lost in the waters below. Arms of experience grasped the nets, spread them and deftly launched them in perfect flight. Again, they slapped the surface of the water as they had 100 times the night before. A thousand times maybe. This time, however, it was different.

Backlighting
Instantly, there was a slight tug. Then the nets were seized and sent wildly convulsing. The pull was overwhelming, catching the strength and experience of even the most seasoned fisherman off guard. Strained arms were etched with protruding veins. Faces were flushed red. The boat listed under the weight as nets were hoisted to the surface. Drawing against the collective resistance, the surface was broken in an explosive torrent of foaming water and flailing fish. The morning sun caught and threw the first silver glint of hundreds of fish, reflected riotously in the churning waters. The water was agitated, surging white and frothy with the multitude of the catch.

Simon Peter was astounded, his mind gaping. The call went out to other boats. They scurried and cast off. Oars plunged deep and hard, frantically pulling against morning's water. A small army of boats surged forward, creating panicked wakes. The catch spilled as a silver torrent into other hulls. Boats creaked, listed and then dropped to the water line, rolling fat with the bulky weight of the catch.

Simon Peter was caught in the breech of trying to draw in nets that were fraying and snapping, while correlating the event in his own mind. For him, it was irreconcilable. It did not match his world or his experience. He was thrust beyond his limited sphere by an event that had occurred in his world, in the very center of it, right in the middle of who he was and what he did. It was other worldly, smacking of something supernatural even. Every sense and sensation inserted it all into the very center of his life to blow him beyond that center. His life was held in sharp relief against something much greater and immeasurably grander than he. He was no longer compared to his world. Now, instantly, he was held up against something infinitely beyond his world. And there, in the stark contrast of a miracle happening in his boat, he saw himself.

Starkly backlit by God, his life was thrust into keen and crippling perspective. The blinding light revealed the thin veneers of his life so much so that he was exposed beyond his ability to comprehend the exposure, much less deal with it. The din of the activity faded as Peter was drawn down into his revealed self. The sea, the boats, the commotion of fellow fishermen: they all disappeared. Simon Peter was fraught with himself, finding himself grappling with the reality of his person.

He turned, stepped, and lunged to the front of the boat. There Jesus had watched the miracle unfold, God enjoying the provision, the message in the provision, and the lives about to be changed by the provision. Peter dropped before Jesus, the proclamation leaping from his lips in stammering honesty. Starkly set against the activity around him, he shouted, Go away from me, Lord, for I am a sinful man! (Luke 5:9 NIV) God had invaded the core of his being, and he had been illuminated against it. There he saw the real self, and he acknowledged what had been exposed. He could not embrace it, so vast was the exposure. Soon the disciples would be named and his would be the first called. It was no wonder.

My World Defining Me

And so I am lulled into the ebb and flow of my life, into the circumstances that swirl in variant pools around me. The eddies and rippling waters reflect back to me more of what they are than who I really am. And I blindly accept those reflections as me, allowing myself to become impoverished in the surrender of acceptance. It is when God steps into the middle of my world that, what I took for God, I find not to be God or of God. It is when He seats himself dead center, squarely at ground zero that I am inoperably exposed. It is here that something vastly superior is held up against who I have defined myself to be and what I have settled for.

Too often my own light is borrowed, reflected off of variant events around me, much like the moon borrowing its light from the sun and reflecting back what does not belong to itself. My life is backlit by weak imitations that reflect things that are not their own, backlighting my life by anemic events that reflect a light so washed out that the landscape of my life is hardly perceptible. This I eventually take for light, the eyes of my soul having become so unaccustomed to real light that its absence is no longer comprehended. I then settle for vagueness as this kind of light provides little more than that. All the while, the profound challenges and wild passions lay a silent captive to the deep shadows that never surrender their contents to whatever light I bring – until my life is backlit.

The Hopeful Shock

The shock of being backlit by Jesus is in the instantaneous awareness that it brings: immediate illumination of everything, stark and clear. Such is the light that the light itself brazenly defines all the aspects of who I am, leaving no room to ponder or stew over them myself. The moment would be robbed otherwise, being something less than wholly divine. To be backlit by Jesus is to fully see and fully comprehend all at once. All that is left for me is to embrace the truth vividly set before me – or squander the moment in denial. More times than I can explain, I have rushed to the front of the boat, prostrated myself before Him, and begged Him leave because I am faced with the horror of myself; my disgust with myself clearly barring my relationship with Him. Inevitably, every time, He looks beyond what I cannot. He sees who I am versus what I have become, delineating the difference in vivid starkness so clear I cannot stand before myself. And then He calls the authentic me, thought bedeviled and helpless, to works beyond my comprehension when all I want is for Him to leave. And it is in the angst of desperately wanting to flee set against His hold on me that I am held against myself and am drawn into phenomenal growth.

Making a Habit of the Light

And so I go fishing with Jesus every day. Fishing for men? Yes. But also that kind of fishing that repeatedly backlights my life against the majesty of God. It is placing myself in His presence while fighting every urge not to do so. It is also readying me for the poignant realization that I am not what I presume to be and being with Jesus will highlight that every time. It is not His disappointment in me; it is my own disappointment in myself. I want to avoid Him because I want to avoid the pain of personal honesty. But I find an incongruent passion that causes me to leap into the boat because I know the joy of being honest before Jesus and what He does with that. And I am constantly, repeatedly and forever changed.

People continued to mill about me, but they had vanished in the midst of the deep thought and emotional turmoil that beset me. I turned to Darren, who was meandering off to some unknown destination – much like his life. I reached out and touched his shoulder. He stopped and staggered a bit as he turned to look at me, his body long worn beyond grace and dexterity of movement. Sparking eyes set deep in worn sockets met mine, shocking me into the realization that I did not have that sparkle. I paused tentatively. Can I see your fish? I stammered. Although a rare treasure, he instantly placed it in my hands without hesitation or forethought. He unabashedly shared the wealth of his life in a simple gesture, freely giving to a soul that needed what he had found. He handed to me what he had grasped. I needed the authenticity of his faith and the deep conviction in whose light my own pathetic belief system shrank and ran.

Such treasures often come in simple packages, like Darren. Their simplicity is their security, as few would look there. Few look there because few lend their eyes to simplicity. Those who do look are not out to rob or pillage the treasure, but rather seek it as a precious gift that no one can hoard or hold by oneself. It is bigger than one individual. It is to be savored, drawn fully into oneself and then left to enrich the next passerby. Hidden away in the Darrens of the world, God has deposited His light, set to explode into any life that is so daring and so desperate as to engage the light in simple places.

I held his plastic fish, turning it this way and that, drawing down into its plastic and paint as had Darren, trying to draw out of it what he had. I'm going to hang it in my house, he blurted. I don't have anything on one wall. It's all white. Just white, that's all. And I'm going to hang it right in the middle, he said. A barren wall – like his life. His faith was hung right in the middle of it. And I thought, how totally appropriate and how absolutely wonderful.

I handed the plastic fish back to him. I'm going to go home right now and hang it up! he said with electric excitement.

As he turned to shuffle away, I called after him and said, Thanks, Darren. There was no response. He hadn't heard me. He was engulfed in the symbol of his faith, a captive to his mad love affair with his God and his fish. Other people still mingled about me, but I no longer desired what they offered. As Darren stepped into the passenger seat of a waiting car, I realized I wanted what he had. I wanted a plastic fish. I wanted a vibrant faith. I wanted to be consumed with God as was this disheveled man, to have all of that hanging in the center of my life. And he had backlit my life in such a way to show me the terrible deficits I had.

I can still see that fish in my mind. It is a clear and vivid reminder of my faith; of following Jesus; of that to which he calls me. Being reminded of that by an event that backlit my life, I could truly see my life. And so, Darren, if some day you read this, I simply want to say what you didn't hear that day: Thank you!

Pondering Point
It is easy to become engulfed and enamored by our worlds. We allow them to shape us, lowering us to a sense of inferiority or raising us to a sense of superiority. Either way, we lose the authenticity of a relationship with Jesus Christ; needing some event in our lives that will hold us up against Him, allowing us, in that encounter, to see our true selves as we are backlit against Him. It raises or crushes us, whatever we might need, either way, bringing us back to authenticity in Christ.

A Thought
- How far have I drifted from Jesus?
- Has there been an event that backlit my life, and what did it illustrate?
- If I have not had one, am I willing to ask God to give me one?
- What have I done with the insights of that event?

Chapter 4

Converging With My Loss

Life intersects us at times in such ways there is no rationale. Events unwind inexplicably, bringing with them a devastation that infuses paralysis. Futility arises and is confirmed in our inability to perceive even the thinnest apparition of good in these events. We squint deeply, the eyes of our hearts and souls intensely attempting to discern some shred of good that gives the bad even the smallest sense of rationale, providing desperate evidence that life is more than random circumstance given free reign to victimize our souls at its own whim.

Yet, often we are unable to detect even the most subtle rhyme or reason, hoping for some rationale that would give meaning to the hell we're in, that would give us something to hold onto in the funnel cloud of anarchy that has ravaged the landscape of our lives. We are desperate for something that would allow us to scan the senseless devastation that lies strewn to the horizon of our lives and be able to say that there is a purpose to it all, that chaos is not the final determiner or irrevocable end of our existence. It is something that would suggest the goodness of God in circumstances that scream both the absence of Him and His goodness. In those most terrible of moments, these are things we are utterly desperate for. Such was her journey.

Three Losses for Amy
A young adult, she had come seeking counsel. Hers was a triple loss. Her life was seemingly ravaged beyond hope of repair. Hurricanes of horror had slammed their enraged centers into the shore of her life – three times in succession. The horrors having passed and drifted inland, the wreckage

of her life lay strewn and pulverized, extending out farther than she could bear to look. The splintered debris lapped the shorelines of her life on incessant waves of interminable grief. She had been laid waste by the fury of life unleashed without restriction, restraint or remorse. The landscape of her life lay utterly unrecognizable.

She sat a mass of devastated humanity, emotionally buckled on my sofa. Torrents of tears were absorbed in a handful of tissues clutched in trembling hands that didn't know what to do with themselves. Deep sobbing represented the last and only thing she knew to do or could do. Teetering on the black abyss of suicide, she had peered over, and as impossible as she would have ever thought it to be, she found its dark chasm preferable to the landscape of wreckage that lay around her. Suicide would be a journey from which life was irrevocably snuffed out and from which no return was possible. And therein lay the compelling incentive to step into the chasm: It would all be mercifully ended. Leaning ever precariously into the pull of the abyss, she had sought me for counseling before allowing its black gravity to send her into a full freefall. She came for hope, for some flicker. Immediately, I realized the holocaust that sat before me.

Two of Three Losses
The shots had come hidden in a hopeless night: a toxic stew of mental illness, life and lethargy blended with marital conflict, alcohol and a loaded revolver. Police reports indicated her stepfather shot his wife, Amy's mother. One bullet was carefully placed in her head to insure the efficiency and permanency of the slug. It was decisive. Apparently, he wasted no time turning the very same weapon on himself, and then he fired a second time just as efficiently. It was over in less than 30 seconds, but it would reverberate down the concourse of Amy's life forever.

A Third Loss
There was another suicide of sorts, however. Not immediate like the one that had leapt out of a hopeless night and then dissipated just as quickly into its stealthy darkness. Those kinds of suicides are easily identifiable because of their immediacy. This one was a slow suicide, like the types so many of us live out not knowing it. It ends in death just the same. It is designed to kill us, but it simply takes longer to get the job done and so we dub it living when it's the very same process that occurred hidden in the hopeless night.

Out of the pain of a murder/suicide, Amy would search for a father who had long abandoned her, turning to him to elicit some morsel of solace. Eventually, she found him, abjectly lost in a cultural morass of alcohol and drugs, a recluse engulfed by the morbidity of senseless self-perpetuated destruction. His instrument of suicide was not a gun, but the slower death of variant substances, both legal and illegal, that did what that single slug did, only slowly enough that all of death's morbid stages were grotesquely highlighted in a manner missed in the immediacy of a shot to the head. He was physically alive, but dead in every other respect. She turned to him, tentatively reaching for a sustaining arm in the gale-force winds that raged around her.

With trembling fingers, she placed a telephone call to a father who was likewise a stranger, living out a distant existence 1,000 miles away, both geographically and emotionally. Having stumbled – dazed, bloodied and maimed – out of the savagery of the suicidal storm that had swept down the shoreline of her life, she thought he might, for once, pity her and be the father he never had been. Even if he were to be a father for only the briefest of moments, simply saying a few things that had even the most minute bits of fatherhood scattered somewhere within them, it would be enough.

Instead, she was met with words slurred by alcohol, leaving only the barest recognition of a voice from a distant past. She strained to correlate the incoherence with the father whose well-worn memories lay rooted in a distant past rendered foggy by time. Barely had the conversation taken shape before a drunken rebuff erupted on the other end. A history thought to be long gone and forever relegated to the annals of the past leapt into the present. His words were calloused and vile, wrapping his rejection of her in toxic trappings. Feelings of abandonment surged out from her past in the form of a slammed receiver and engulfed her in a tsunami of horror. Holding a phone gone dead, drowning in an empty dial tone that seemed to mock her hopes for a father, she collapsed into a heaving heap on the floor of her apartment and sobbed for two, dark hours: a third loss.

Now, here she was in my office, attempting to string together the events in a way that allowed her to somehow still believe that God was good and had a plan of some sort, that the insanity had some redeeming thread hidden away somewhere in the ravaging folds of its black fabric. Her pain was steeped in her inability to do exactly that. She was dying. There would be a fourth death if I failed. There would be a fourth if God didn't show up.

Another Loss

Two crowds moved toward a healing collision. One headed south from coastal Capernaum with the Son of God amidst a swirling mass of mesmerized admirers. Another moved north, spilling out through the chalky white basalt arches of a city gate bleached by an unrelenting sun, scoured by gritty winds and stuccoed rough with pain.

A funeral bier and a grieving mother set a cadence slogged in the mire of despair. Death had come as the indomitable thief and had pillaged freely. Its thirst not satiated the first time, it returned to take the widow's son after it had taken her husband. She was bent twice by death. Stumbling and then collapsing, she fell faint into the sturdy arms of those who escorted her in a sullen procession, punctuated by the plaintive wails of the grieving that accentuated the silence of death. She herself was living death.

Off in the distance, just beyond the edge of a horizon, shimmering in the heat of a day rubbing itself warm, there walked a prophet. His cadence was set and measured by the defeat of death, creating a very different tempo. He had just vied with death in the dying body of an obscure servant of a centurion. So powerful was He that death had been thwarted from a distance. To the contrary, despite pleadings long into the dark night of the soul, this woman had surrendered a son to death. Each were set to meet standing on the opposite ends of life, closing in from opposite directions on the hard-packed dust of a thin road that would direct the two to each other. Two fluid masses were set to merge in an historical convergence, one desperately needing what the other possessed, not knowing a convergence with God's power was about to offset death's power. Flowing, they converged along the dusty road of grief that wound through a mother's heart.

An only son and a husband, the sting of death – twice. First there was a husband's funeral with a cold brier and a grieving crowd just like this one. The same road was being walked again. They passed the same bleached basalt arches, their chalky whiteness mimicking the pallor of death. The footprints were still fresh across the dusty expanse of her heart. Her son had assumed the vacated headship, providing financially and representing the family in the social and religious life of the community. He likely postponed marriage out of his obligation to the family. And now, he passed, one death but a multiple loss: a son, a provider, a seed for a next generation that would never be. She was inconsolable, and she was drowning when the two waves converged.

Word filtered back to Jesus. Death, ever persistent, was about its dark business with its black handiwork laid out in an approaching funeral bier. Jesus had thwarted it only days earlier in the life of a menial servant. Recoiling in the rage of defeat, death had raced ahead of Him, seizing a life once and a family twice as if to exact revenge and retribution on this Messiah. Now it flagrantly waved its work in His face.

 She is a widow. Jesus paused and recalled with vivid clarity the furrowed lines of pain etched across his own mother's face at the death of Joseph, His father. The spastic convulsion of caustic grief wrenched his mother at death's visitation to His own family. Her face was awash in tears. Burying her head in His chest, she murmured the repeated and plaintive *why* that echoed the crippling disorientation and abrupt finality of death. Somehow, He was closer to the widow's grief. An only son as was He. The provider of this family, as Jesus was to His. Jesus saw His own past in the widow's face and in the oddity of their shared humanity. He saw His future in the funeral bier. His heart went out to her as His choice to become exactly that which He had created allowed Him to so deeply identify with His own creation. He was both God and His creation simultaneously. He quickened His pace. The waves converged.

My Funeral Briers
Funeral biers frequently tread the thin, dusty roads of my heart. Sometimes, their contents are clear, known and understandable. More often than not, they are painfully indiscernible.

The fingers of my heart tremble. They draw across the coarse boards, hoping for the slightest pulse, the most subtle semblance of warmth that would refute what I know to be true. They are familiar, too familiar. My life clouds with thunderheads of grief. My heart groans. My spirit wails in deep convulsions at yet another death that seems nothing more than a cruel act that gives life some sort of morbid pleasure. That life seeks some form of sadistic entertainment at my expense. When life has had its fill and is content, it will then allow this devastation, whatever it has been, to destroy me, for I have been expended in the provision of the entertainment.

Often I cry at the senselessness of it all. Sometimes I am inconsolable. Often I am desperate. Incapacitated, I stumble alongside the bier, holding whatever it is that has died this time, wondering when all these deaths will kill me. I wonder how I will survive this loss in light of all the other losses. I'm paralyzed by the fear of what loss might be next. How soon will I again walk this dusty road? How many other funeral biers will there be? Will I survive another? When will I be that thing in the brier? I saw that in Amy. Her eyes softly bespoke exactly that. Her heart screamed it, and I felt it, its power thrusting me back in my chair and sending my clinician mind spinning for some answer to that which sometimes has no answer. Often there is no answer to death, only a response based on forced surrender

Life from Death
But there was a convergence coming along this very road, this same road that seemed so intolerable. It was a road of resignation that blew only the dust of defeat in parched swirling eddies across graves where hope was interred and forever entombed. There was a convergence set for her road, coming toward her, toward me and toward you, a convergence with a man of sorrows ... familiar with suffering (Isaiah 53:3 NIV). He was coming, closing, constantly drawing nearer when we would suspect nothing on this terribly desolate road other than pain. Word filtered to Him. Our pain resonated with His. He had experienced our pain, but perfectly so. He had walked beside the biers, but He had also been laid in them. The difference: He rose out of them with the felt futility of every bier having been undermined in His resurrection. He quickened His pace. His heart goes out to you, to me, and to all the Amys stumbling through their grief as they tread the dusty roads of broken hearts.

Don't cry (Luke 7:13 NIV). The widow had every reason to cry – as do we. She had every reason not to cry but did not know it. Both crowds momentarily converged, blending into a single solid mass drawn around a solitary funeral bier. Stillness settled, and the crowd became hushed.

No miracle had been requested. Perhaps it was not known that one was possible. Perhaps loss can be so scorching that restoration was inconceivable, being thrust out to the margins of the mind and shoved into an emotional abyss. Perhaps loss can be bigger than our ability to comprehend it and therefore, vaster than our ability to conceptualize a solution to it. Perhaps!

Jesus paused and stared into vacant eyes of a worn woman left hollow from the incomprehensible nature of loss, the thievery having stolen the spark that sets mankind apart from all else in creation. That spark of life was gone, and He was grieved. He turned from the widow, eyed the bier and squinted in soft determination. Coarse boards. The symbol of surrender carrying the thing surrendered, representing the utter helplessness of mankind to redeem loss, to choose something other than surrender.

Then … a squared grimace of determination mixed with a slight smile of pending liberation set itself in His features. Eyes glinting, Jesus moved toward the coffin, the crowd parting in His advance. Confidence marked each step. He halted. Any hesitation absent, He reached out and deliberately touched the bier, gently running His fingers across its embalmed coarseness. Oblivious to the pallbearers and the crowd, His heart was determined and His focus concise. With words, firm, confident and yet soft, He drew a breath and said, Young man, I say to you, get up! (Luke 7:14 NIV)

Immediately a slight, shallow breath was drawn on the heels of the one drawn by Jesus to utter the command of life. There was a pause as if what was seen was a mirage, a projection of a corporate hope embraced by all gathered there, but being nothing more than a projection. Then the next breath – deeper this time. Then another pause. Ashen skin was rubbed warm, his complexion deepening into soft fleshy tones. Muscles drew a stiff arm across the rising chest. The body shifted slightly as if stretching itself awake from sleep. Pallbearers, suddenly balancing the shifting weight, were lost in an emotional abyss, their minds frozen in the grip of the impossible being made possible.

A hand rose and clasped the boards, secured a tight grip with wrapped fingers, and the body was pulled upright. A gasp raced deep through the crowd, followed quickly on its heels by the electrifying reality of what is transpiring. Grave clothes unraveled; their loosed ends softly fluttered as they were caught by a gentle breeze. The man's hand traced a tremulous path up the side of his head until he found the end of the cloth. He then peeled the wraps off his face in sweeping circular motions that became increasingly ecstatic with each rotation. The last wrap fell away; the crowd gasped; the son shaded his eyes from the surge of blinding sunlight; and with intensity, he scanned the crowd. A murmuring swell surged across the throng. His eyes landed on Jesus. Ever intent, Jesus smiled, held out a hand and escorted the man to life.

Immediately he was conversant, possibly recounting the glories of heaven to Jesus or perhaps recognizing Jesus as the visiting God descended from that place. Likely amazed at his own return, he gave praise to God. Arms outstretched, he shouted, Mother, Mother! We do not know. The text does not say. But he talked, and much he had to say.

The funeral was over, but the crowd had not grasped that yet, not entirely. But it was indeed over. The text states that Jesus gave him back to his mother (Luke 7:15 NIV). The terminology is reminiscent of the return of a prisoner of war or a captive released, the place of captivity having been invaded by force and the prisoner abducted to freedom: released, returned and fully restored. The response of the mother is unrecorded. She was likely hysterical, as would be most of us. It is probable that she touched him with pensive hands, hugged deeply, drew back to look with amazement, to verify, touched and seized him yet again. A mix of wild joy wed with a sense of impossibility that told her that what she knew to be true could not be true. She had to allow her senses to repeatedly take in the unfathomable reality before her in order to know it to be true.

The bier was empty. A dead man stood on a dusty road outside basalt gates rendered a warm mauve from a setting sun. Pallbearers stood beside an empty bier turned on its side as if it had spilled its contents – for it had. Hope was reclaimed from the abyss. The dead man stood in a pile of unraveling grave clothes.

The crowd condensed toward the center and consolidated around the young man, having to do their own verifying. The sun, bright and vibrant, warmed the landscape. The crowd eventually turned toward home. No burial today. Mourning turned to celebration, and Jesus moved on.

Coming to Our Biers
And so He comes to our coffins. When we see no recourse to this, yet

another loss, He comes down that hopeless road, looking at us with compassion of eternal proportions. He says, Don't cry. With a grimace of determination mixed with a slight smile of pending liberation, Jesus moves toward our many coffins. Confidence marks each step. He halts. Without hesitation, He touches them; gently He runs His fingers across their coarseness, oblivious to the frigid distractions that death brings with it. His heart is determined and His focus concise. With words, firm, confident, but soft, He says, I say to you, get up! (Luke 7:14 NIV) And life is restored: our lives -- yours, mine and anyone who would risk hope. The funeral is indeed over, and often we don't really realize it. What had been stolen is given back to us, and we stand in utter amazement, sometimes hysterical that what was lost to us has been given back. Eventually we turn toward home. No burial today. Mourning turned to celebration. And we are stunned by His work in our lives.

Amy's Restoration
Sometimes we don't know we're dead until we're made alive. Sometimes things in our lives have to die so that we, by holding ourselves up against the loss, can see our own deadness. In the grander scheme of things, it is not necessarily about the return of that which has died. Rather, it is about seeing how that which has died perpetually maintained my own living death and that, in its absence, it no longer holds me.

In the end, it was Amy who was in those biers, not her mother, stepfather or father. All were dysfunctional and had deeply scarred her life. She was the accumulation of the sordid actions and self-centered choices that had been spilled out upon her for year after devastating year. Heartless neglect and sadistic abuse had merged into an acidic mix that had dissolved her soul, rendering her life a zombie-like apparition. She thought herself to be living, but she was dead, any spark of life having long been extinguished by these three people before she was old enough to know what that spark was. Their actions had put her in a bier decades earlier. Their death was her resurrection.

It was Amy who was in those biers. Three other deaths had put her there. Therapy would be long and arduous. The bier and the funeral procession would traverse the dusty roads of her soul for quite some time. Sometimes life's journey is not about the miraculous as much as it's about Jesus in the mundane. In time, however, there was a convergence along her road.

Unexpectedly and shockingly, she drew her first real breath, sat up for the first time, groped to unfurl the grave clothes, and squinted into the light of life and the face of Jesus. She was 26, and she was alive for the first time. Today, her bier is finally empty.

Pondering Point

Things die in and around us. We relegate ourselves to the losses, sometimes railing against them, raising questions about life, about God, and about the validity of life and living. We presume that death implies burial, the action assuming the permanence of loss. We relegate that part of ourselves or life as forever vanquished to thievery. The resultant diminishment and reduction of life is seemingly hopeless. It is but stolen hopes and pilfered promises. However, Jesus is the Master at seizing what is dead and resurrecting the lost, bringing something immeasurably grander into our lives than that which was lost. He stands ready to walk beside your biers, whatever they might be, whenever they might be.

A Thought
- What are my biers?
- How many have I relegated to the past that I might reclaim through Jesus?
- Am I willing to invite Him to my biers, knowing that my life will be radically different because I made that choice?

Chapter 5
Aside with God

Dean was deaf. It was that simple, but it was inordinately complex at the same time. Life can have its sinkholes. Sometimes there's a bunch of them, enough to cause a broad and crippling implosion. Life then becomes a litany of foggy responses to trauma where we move zombie-like through whatever the day or the moment holds. There is no forward movement in times like these. It's about survival. Soon survival becomes the norm where we strive to survive for the sake of survival itself. Life becomes meaningless other than getting through the day to fight the meaninglessness that will face us again tomorrow.

Dean was deaf. Plus, he was mentally retarded. Tender and kind, compassionate and soft, he was the byproduct of the sinkholes that had scattered themselves all around his life. In the end, it all collapsed and he retreated into his deafness and his mental retardation, finding there some seclusion. He sat along the roadside of life, watching some of it go by and ignoring the rest. He surrendered to isolation. The world being held at arms' length, he barricaded himself deep within, out of reach of anything. He was a treasure lost.

He had never mastered his deafness. Some lean into their disability and shape it to serve them. He never did. Quite the opposite, he never touched it at all. Sign language and the reading of lips never broke him out of the prison that deafness had thrust him into: that place so deep no one could reach. He was somehow held inside with the world kept outside. Each could see the other from their respective vantage points, but neither could bridge the gap nor plumb the depths.

A Conviction of Greatness
Life sometimes convinces us there is so much more to something or someone, even though we can't see it. We engage that thing or that person with a certainty that there lies within something profound despite the fact it's hidden entirely. It seems we walk circles around them, looking and probing for some crack or tear that will grant us entrance to the riches within. There emerges a dogged persistence about it all because we dare not bypass what lies within, even though it's held away from us.

That was Dean. He was a kid I could not let go of even though there was nothing to hold onto. His mild mental retardation put him even further away. He was a young man of riches unearthed that always provoked me back to him. He was frustrating and abrasive at times, being unable to break through his own deafness and reach up and out to anything outside of himself. Because he couldn't, he reinforced his isolation from the inside out, pushing everything away so he would have a sense that he was in control. I suppose it gave him a sense of power over his deafness, a power that reduced the sense of deep victimization and loss.

I didn't choose to be relentless with this kid. I had no choice. Sometimes what you see in another is far too convincing and too terribly compelling to let it go – even when you meet with nothing more than rejection and walls. And walls there were, thick and fortified. I found myself in relentless pursuit and then disappointed into withdrawal, only to do it all over again because this kid was somehow just too precious to let go of. He needed to hear, maybe not with his ears, but at least with his heart. I prayed God would pull Dean aside and unlock something that would open him up.

Deaf to Life
Rejection and scorn, there was an assumption of sin about him. The world was loudly silent. Something was missing. Life was indeed an orchestra, full and complete, absolutely masterful but absolutely soundless. The pieces for which life was created were soundless in an inescapable silence that drowned out everything else. Notes and scores that were casually written across the faces of friends; that were penned in the raucous flamboyance across bustling open air markets; that found subtle notation in droning bees gently drifting from blossom to awaiting blossom all gave the faintest hints of the melodies they illustrated, but the sounds were never there.

The haunting call of myriad geese aloft. The pounding surf throwing itself against a forever beach. The fingers of the wind rustling through listless treetops. The roll of a distant summer thunderstorm on a humid horizon. The sound of silence as a pause amidst the notes and scores, not an absence of them. Entombed in a vacuum of deafening silence, the orchestra had always played soundless for him, playing vigorously, but silently. He was deaf, and he was alone.

To attempt to interact, to engage, to try to participate in a world you can't hear leaves you ever outside that world. His lips were slow and drawn; the words were ill-formed, trying to wrap themselves around voice and syntax he had never heard. He tried to do what he couldn't conceive and could much less imagine. His words were slurred, distorted, verbally twisted and linguistically bent, readily inviting and successfully garnering ridicule, mockery and confusion from those who lived in the world of sound. His was an existence forced out onto the fringes of life, exiled there in a lonely land where silence is a hated but forever companion. There was no breech in the wall to slip back through in order to touch humanity, so as to belong to something other than the silence. Rejection by others was based on errant assumptions that were elevated as full-fledged fact, rendering him an outcast on the falsest of premises. Rejection and silence are both isolating, the difference is that one is a choice; the other is chance. What they have in common is that the one upon whom they fell chose neither. A full emasculation of everything it is to be human: This is what it is to be deaf and mute. And so his life went.

There was a rumor. It was a distant murmuring unheard by deaf ears, but caught by others: Jesus was in the Decapolis. Had those around him tired of his dependency, these friends of the deaf man, or did they care for him? Was he little more than an object that could be used to entice a miracle of this prophet, a ploy for a cheap thrill? The text is unclear. The motive is foggy. But they took the deaf mute to Jesus. Not of his own accord, for there is no hint of self-determination or self-initiation. He had no idea of the possibility of being ushered into the world of sound, a world he knew nothing of, a world alien to an inhabitant of the fringes of that world. Yet there were those few on the inside who saw far enough outside to catch a shadowy glimpse of those who lived lives isolated beyond pain. They would not settle for deafness and isolation as the sum total of what life held. They reached out and pulled the outsiders in.

And so the rumor drew them to Jesus. Soon the embedded mass was found. Ushered by these friends, the deaf man pressed through the crowd, the small entourage cut a swath through a fluid array of assorted humanity that swelled and eddied. The clamor of a world of needs simultaneously sought relief, healing and some shred of hope. The crowd swirled around Jesus as if in the grip of the undertow of all creation, an irresistible current from which all other currents found their sole source. Passing through a cultural morass, the deaf man was drawn toward the center.

The aged, stooped and shuffling in the grip of long years, wandered about in a cloudy curiosity. Children darted in and out. The blind – groping, stretching trembling arms outward, substituting touch for sight, sound for vision – made their way to Jesus. Those with crutches, crude and weather-worn, with primitive prosthetics, sought a miracle. A cripple, his fingers clawing the arid soil, dragging useless appendages and tattered garments that trailed in the talcum dirt, drew forward. Limp in his mother's arms lay an infant, the pallor of death awash across the face of newborn life, his skin hues of suffocating purple; his mother standing on tiptoe, stretching her neck to catch a glimpse of something, anxiously groped toward the center of the mass. It was all silence to the man: alive, vibrant, wild even, but deathly silent. From his vantage point, the drama was only partly revealed.

Pressing onward and inward, it was more of the same: shifting layers of broken humanity, the curious, the destitute, rich and poor alike. He moved past the final layers, and there stood a man of silent stature, yet infinitely above it. The nucleus of the swirling mass of people and their needs was deafening in its silence. His back was to them. Slightly stooped, His hands gently rested on the shoulders of an elderly woman. The look of astonishment was set in her eyes and splashed across her face. A worn cane lay abandoned at her feet. Something unusual had transpired. It was immediately clear there was compassion in His touch, His stance, His mannerisms. A parting word and He turned.

His gaze shifted, panning the crowd. Mussing the hair of a playful child, both smiled deeply, invading the heart of the other: a divine intersection. Another step and He was drawn to the outstretched arms of an ecstatic infant. He moved toward her, His face alive with love and aflame with anticipation. To squeals of laughter, He took her, held her high, pulled her to His chest, ran His hand across a misshapen leg, and it was straight. In the convergence of two souls, He drew her deeply to His face. And then He handed her back to an elated parent – whole. It was too much for words, too inexplicable. Who was this?

Before the answer could be formulated, Jesus was drawn to the pleas of those who had brought the deaf mute, pleas the deaf man could not hear. The man, this Jesus, stepped toward them, devoting His attention to those who brought the man, discerning, listening. He then turned intense eyes and fastened His gaze on the mute, His eyes deep, thoughtful and focused. A soft but chiseled spirit enamored the crowd and drew the deaf man. It was all a terrible contradiction of commanding power and gentle softness. Jesus' eyes had the breath of infinity behind them, being so easy to become lost in until Jesus took his arm, gestured, and began to move out of the crowd. God was afoot, the Creator of the universe in intentional motion. It was all terrifying, but exhilarating at the same time.

A fluid mass of humanity parted a second time, but from the inside out. Shifting layers of broken humanity sliced a swath to the edge of the mass. Purposeful, Jesus breeched the fringes of the crowd with a man who had been forced onto the fringes of life, isolating a man isolated by deafness. In a moment, the crowd was behind, their voices falling into a distant murmur. Those who advocated his healing were absent. Suddenly, inexplicably, he was alone – with God.

Ears and tongue, the world was drawn in through one with the self being released through the other. They both engaged in a partnership of exchange, drawing in and letting out, drawing in the world to process it and releasing it back with part of the person attached; adding to life, flavoring it, affixing yet another unique note to the chorus of the ages – contributing. Here, in the world of the deaf, this dance was never initiated. He had been isolated from the world and to the world.

Drawing the man, Jesus sought isolation. It was within isolation that isolation would be broken. One on one, God and man were in relationship, echoing back to a lost garden. The Creator and the created were rectifying lost creation. They walked past the rancor and raucous of an open air market filled with bartering and bantering, scales and sweeping gestures; around scurrying children; past stray dogs milling close to tables spread with red meats. A pair of centurions laden with weaponry walked past in the service of oppression. Passing priests in ceremonial robes stepped in pompous cadence.

And then, an unexpected turn into a vacant alley. Basalt stones created a manmade canyon. The sun, finding scant room to watch, cast angled rays, canting itself to catch the miracle. The din of the open air market and the jostling of the vendors, the world was muted and put at a distance, fading into the background.

Then, a miracle wrought with gestures so familiar to the mute. Gestures were the very means of understanding and navigating his world. Jesus was not a God interacting in mystery, but in intimacy. There were no methods cloaked with indiscernible actions. All was simple, direct and familiar: fingers in ears and a touch of the tongue. Saliva ... a sharing of self as a participant in the miracle, not as a distant entity cloaked beyond recognition in immutability. It was believed to have had a curative quality, a belief entirely fictional in nature. However, the symbolism of the act provided a needed vehicle that outweighed the myth of the act itself, and so Jesus chose to use myth as a means for a miracle, a miracle done in the simple language of the man's isolated world to obliterate his isolation.

And then there was something for Jesus Himself. Plus, there was something the deaf man could not hear or participate in. Jesus looked up to heaven. There was the sigh of the God whose love eliminated His ability not to feel, a reflection of both His heart and that of His Father's. It seems the lethal weight of the private pain of the God grieving over His creation could only be escaped by virtue of His divinity. It was likely the plaintive moan of God embracing the awful reality of fallen mankind as manifest in this single mute life. It was an exhaustion so great it could only have its root in an infinite understanding of the extent of the loss. In that alley, He met the need of one. A few days later, He would meet the need of thousands with a scant seven barley loaves and a few small fish. A few months after that, He would meet the need of all mankind and the cumulative pain for which He sighed. He would not be sandwiched between the walls of an alley, but between two crosses and two worlds. However, He met the need of that moment.

"Be opened!" (Mark 7:34 NIV) It was not just his ears, but also his life

– as no miracle is excluded solely to the obvious. "Be opened!" He was free to live fully, to hear in perfect pitch the richness of the notes and measures, the scores of life and living. Jesus took a step back and watched life unfold as the miracle reverberated far beyond the center as when a stone is dropped in a mirrored pool, sending ripples far beyond the point of impact. Something happened. An alien experience transpired for which the man had no point of correlation. Sounds began to filter through. The orchestra swelled. The void filled.

Suddenly he heard the crunch of gravel beneath his feet, shifting his weight again and again to reproduce the sound his stunned and hungry mind had never imagined. The barking of a dog floated in from afar, the source of the sound and everything that defined it entirely unknown. Birds darted overhead in tangles of wild flight, cheeps and chirps synchronizing their feathered mass. His own breath. And then words, the first ever heard, were annunciated clearly, perfectly and concisely. His own voice! The cycle was now complete.

Jesus stood silently, giving the man room and time to embrace the wonder of the moment, that miracles become freeing and claustrophobic at the same time, opening up entirely new venues that are often bigger than our ability to embrace. Time was needed to reorient himself to the miracle of a life restored. Perhaps Jesus saw in this man, this deaf mute, the liberation that the cross would extend to billions. It may be that the individual miracles, like this one, allowed Jesus to foresee in a single face what the cross would do. He saw not miracles that would eventually fall to the deterioration of frail bodies and the eventuality of death, but miracles that would be eternally fresh. I wonder if it might have been these moments that allowed Him to endure the long moments on a lonely cross.

"Don't tell anyone." The words seemed irrational and inexplicable. The world of sounds brings with it responsibility to the world it unveils. Miracles bring with them accountability to both the Restorer and what has been restored. A relationship with God brings obedience, the responsibility to act on faith when that action appears irrational, contrary, odd or plainly wrong. "Don't tell anyone." But containment failed. The measure of the miracle was larger than the measure of the man to contain it. But that is God interacting. What He does is always bigger than us and bigger than our ability to contain it. Our faith may be big enough to elicit a miracle, but our faith is seldom large enough to embrace it until time permits us to grow into it. The miracle spills out and over the edges of our lives. Jesus took his arm, gestured and began to move out of the alley and into life.

Aside in an Alley

He pulls me aside at times and isolates me in my isolation. He places creation aside and draws me to a secluded place, away from the crowds that surround me and the world that has so often thrust me to its fringes. And often I am afraid to be there because I am confused and frightened to be one on one with God. I would much prefer to have Him heal me or intersect my life in the companionship of others; or as part of something larger within which I can meld; or better yet, at a comfortable distance. But one on one in some alley in my life, secluded with God? Sequestered with the Creator? It is both terrible and wonderful.

To have Him connect with me intimately in that place of isolation? God coming to me? He comes not just in proximity, but in language and in the raw essence of my being, stepping into my isolation and speaking to me there. He does not stand outside of it and beckon to me. Coming in, God gently takes my arm and gestures me out of it. He partners with me, and in the partnering, He comes squarely into my isolation to commandeer and rescue me. Cutting through the mass of issues, pain, self-absorption, and self-hatred that surrounds me, He draws me along with Him.

And there, in those isolated alleys of my life, He frees me. God relishes in seeing me come to life and fumbling with this life so new that I have little idea how to hold it. He is as amazed at watching me come to life as He was when He formed Adam from the dust and breathed into his nostrils the breath of life (Genesis 2:7 NIV). It is just as poignant, never being diminished for a God whose love for His creation rages undiminished. God is always revealing in the timeless wonder that creation can only exist if it is constantly creating. "He has done everything well ..." (Mark 7:37 NIV). Harkening to yet another statement ... "And God saw that it was good" (Genesis 1:10 NIV). In that alley, God was creating all over again – as He does.

Dean's Alley

It was all experimental, but the doctors said the surgery might restore Dean's hearing. He was not enthused. Dean walked through the process more like a laboratory rat that had no idea of what was happening or what the possible outcome might mean. He was lethargic through it all, demure and distant.

But the day came quite by accident. I turned and there he stood. My first response was to say "hello" out of some prescribed tedium and routine, knowing that he wasn't reading my lips. Sometimes rote and ritual turns life lifeless. It robs us of expectation and hope. I felt that way with Dean.

He simply looked, canting his head a bit and registering something in those crystal blue eyes I had never seen. Sometimes we imagine something so much for so long that, when it's ours, it's both wonderful and terribly different than we had imagined it. I think that was the case for Dean. He had heard my voice. The surgery had worked. For the first time, he had taken in the tone and flavor of the single word I had uttered and found himself awed. He smiled and seemed to wait for more. "Can you hear me?" I asked tentatively, desperately hoping he was no longer locked in and I locked out.

Instantly he grabbed my arm, turned and in the rush of wonder, pulled me down the hall and into his room, pointing at the various objects around us in frantic gestures that I might pronounce what they were. Picture, telephone, window, bed, floor, light, wall, Craig ... It was a young man surging alive with an urgency that flooded the room with a terrific and wonderful energy. He was hearing it all for the first time.

Sometimes you sense you've been put in a place of privilege you are completely and wholly undeserving of. That was where I was that day. God came alongside this young man through the hands of a caring doctor and an experimental surgery. Now I was privileged to stand with him as well, inundated in a tsunami of wonderment and life.

It all went on for days and days. I couldn't wait to see Dean. In indescribable awe, I watched a young man come alive in a way that makes coming alive worth all the pain and disappointment and deafness we have to endure to get there. A miracle came to me through Dean. Deafness was abated in infinitely more ways that simply physical hearing. Dean reminds me of deafness and what it can do to a person and a life. Dean also reminds me of deafness abated when God comes alongside a single life and what that life can then hear.

Repeated Deafness

Unlike the deaf mute and unlike Dean, my deafness and my inability to speak to my world come often. Frequently I need Jesus to put His fingers in my ears and touch my tongue, thrusting an event onto center stage that will do exactly that. Sin, selfishness and the lure of the world renders me deaf and ill-suited to speaking as I should. My condition is pitifully recurrent. God's presence is likewise persistently recurrent. Daily I am in this alley with Him. While I tire of it and find myself sweltering in embarrassment, He never tires. He likes, it seems, these alley encounters. He relishes taking me aside. And I know one day He will take me aside for that final time, that time when I will ascend to a place where deafness and speech deficits will not exist. Their memory will be vanquished. And there, in that place, I will stand eternally before God in perfection with new worlds perpetually opening up to me, the layers constantly parting to reveal something new. His smile and the relish in His face will never be old.

Pondering Point

The loud voices in life, those that clamor for our attention, are most often not the vital voices. The fact that they have to clamor suggests as much. It is the smaller voices: weak, thin and easily drowned out. It is these that tend to be the priceless voices. Their worth is easily lost in the pompous and presumptuous voices that say much but hold little. It is easy to become deaf. And when we are, we miss the precious voices whose worth is immutable.

A Thought

- What am I hearing?
- Is what I'm hearing dictated by what I've chosen to listen to?
- Are these things loud enough to deafen me to other things?
- What is being drowned out? Is God being drown out?

Chapter 6

Judging in the Courtyard

Filth described her well. While it was an apt depiction, it failed to embrace the fullest description of what she was. Some lives seem to be nothing more than a brutal manifestation of the accumulated slag and scum that is left over in the wake of some departed tragedy. These people become the thing life has done to them, being so irreparably identified with their own tragedies they themselves are a living manifestation of all those assorted tragedies. Hers was a life that was already an abysmal collection of untold catastrophes that resulted in filth nearly indescribable. She was only 14.

Susan was of little note as she stepped off the bus that first day of summer camp. She was one of over 100 campers swirling in an arriving mass of anticipation. She had tattered bags and a tattered spirit. Her eyes were set hollow with the effects of a life lived in hatred. Filth and a pervading stench drew her apart from the rest almost instantly. Her soul seemed to reek with a putrid odor that exceeded the smell emanating from her skin and clothing. There was about her an inner ugliness that permeated everything else about her, that had consumed her and had digested whatever shred of good there might have been, effectively leaving the sludge of human goodness now consumed.

Her defense mechanism was so refined it immediately repelled all who drew near, thrusting others so far away she guaranteed her own isolation. The woundedness was so utterly complete the poison of the pain she felt was spewed in venomous rages at anyone who ventured too close. Her self-hatred was effectively projected outward onto anyone who dared draw near physically or emotionally. She seemed as something less than human; something abominable; something terribly horrifying within which any shred of humanity was consumed and utterly lost.

The following week of camp was to be marred by ugly confrontations. Rages. Refusals to shower. Outbursts seething with anger distilled into lethal poison that devastated other hearts, young and old. Physical assaults and violent rages had an insane wildness and a touch of insanity about them. There emerged, at times, something animalistic about her, something very primal that raged unrestrained by reason or rationale. At times, the line between that of a visceral animal and a human being was blurred and terribly ill-defined.

In the end, Susan was isolated in a lone cabin. Her parents refused to come and get her. Her pastor was unwilling and unable to deal with her rages, as her life did not fit neatly into some clean theological rubric. The camp staff gathered to pray for her, but found their prayers ineffective. Some sort of spiritual possession was questioned – and rightly so. She was a monster, a raging pathetic monster that we waited to relieve ourselves of at the close of camp. Such was our judgment of her.

Judging From Fear
Judging is, I think, a manifestation of our own fears. We judge so we might have some sense of control and some feeling of superiority. If we judge that which is before us, we assume we will not become whatever it is we are rendering judgment upon. We set ourselves apart as distinct from that thing or that person with that distinction, somehow convincing ourselves we are different. Judging places us above that which we judge, meaning we will not succumb to it from our elevated position.

We judge because we fear. And because we fear, we are not prone to look deeply. For if we look deeply, we might see ourselves. We might be forced to surrender to the reality that that which we are rendering judgment upon is as much a part of us as it is of the person we are judging. Superficial judgment allows us to bypass our own humanity and live the lie of superiority. The person whom we judge is then sacrificed to our self-serving judgments. Plus, whatever is it God wanted to do in our lives through that person is likewise lost.

Judgment Revealed

It was to be that final night. The next morning a mass of buses and cars would invade the gravel parking lot, snatching up sunburned campers filled with the wild tales of a week's adventures. But that would be the next day. For night had fallen, drawing up a warm blanket of thick summer air across the camp and out beyond the wooded expanse, tucking the world in at each horizon. Crickets sang in a chorus of the night from the deep woods, lulling the day to slumber with their mesmerizing notes. Frogs bellowed thick from a stream that meandered through a wooded ravine down a slight ridge. Their chorus hauntingly rolled up the rise and across the slight meadow. Lightening bugs cast dancing pinpoint pigments of yellow across the shadowy landscape and deep into the tall stands of sleepy timber. The moon had only shaken a sliver of itself awake, mingling with the starry minions. It was the perfect night, soft and subtle. God's creation was melding into perfection.

With the campers bedded down for that final night, I strolled down to the chapel, which was bathed in the soft shadows of night. A few moments with God at the end of a long week seemed so right. Drawn, I ascended the winding dirt and gravel path with the soft crunch of each step muffled by night's thick softness. Slight shadows cut from the thin pastel light of a sleepy moon seemed to whisper something about reverence and what it is to be alone with God.

Another person had thought the same. The outdoor chapel was framed by a wall of river rock that extended muscular granite arms around an expansive gravel floor. Across the gravel expanse, there stood a rock and timber altar with a muscular, rough-hewn cross as a shadowy sentry. Thick timbers supported a vaulted wooden roof spread with broad knotty pine boards. The woods beyond were alive with the night – and she was there.

A shadowy figure knelt at the altar. Her aloneness was poignant, an isolated life kneeling before an altar in a desperate hope of somehow breaking that isolation. The crying was soft and indistinct, muted by her fear of vulnerability. The moment was a manifestation of a broken heart and deeply wounded spirit that had somehow collided with God enough to strike a spark of hope. She was kneeling there, her fingers embedded in the rock altar, hoping this hope would not fail her as had everything else.

We had all seen her as ugly, despicable, the scum of humanity that teetered on the savagery of a wild animal. We wanted nothing more than to see the sun break on the final day of camp and watch her leave both the camp and our lives. To be rid of her. To relegate this vermin back to the hole from which she had crawled. To say we hated Susan was likely excessive. To say we despised her was likely true. And yet, here she was. Broken. The wounded humanity she so vehemently lashed out from was pouring out across that rock and timber altar. Her core was exposed, and I saw her humanity. I had errantly judged it not to be there for fear I would recognize it in myself. Now I saw her brokenness, and in it, I recognized my own.

I feared her, not knowing in that moment what to do, not wanting to do anything out of the fear of behaviors I'd observed and the hatred I'd seen spew from her. But I found myself walking toward her. I had made no conscious decision to do anything. Yet my footsteps were dictated by something wholly other than me. And then I was beside her in the thick darkness; the thick of night; the thick of her night. Without a word spoken, she reached up and took my hand, drawing me down to her side with a force that buckled my knees. She put a trembling arm around me as if the whole of her spirit was leaning its weight on me. I felt, for that brief instance, the intolerable hell of her life. And in that moment, I understood why she was what she was. Her words were to silence the night that surrounded us. Nature drew down into the moment and stood on tiptoe, so it seemed as God reached out from the expanse of that starry night and changed a life.

Her next words set me back, instantly slicing through all the things that had caused me to judge her so harshly and revealed who this really was. She asked, Would you pray with me? Without a word from me, her heart ruptured open in prayer. I never uttered a word. I didn't have to as such an action would have been only an intrusion in that transforming moment. Floodgates surged opened, and a massive reservoir of pain that had accumulated over the incalculable expanse of years and events deluged the darkened chapel. I knelt – stunned. I had diminished her in my judgments, and I experienced my own cleansing in hers. It was a marvelous and privileged moment.

In the end, we spent over an hour kneeling in the gravel, cloaked in a deep summer's night. Her prayers, a lifetime tidal wave of events and circumstances, kept coming. Abuse. Neglect. Drugs. The assorted maladies included hunger, too few clothes, empty birthdays, numerous evictions, the rejection by society that abject poverty brings to a young life, a devastating abortion, and a fathomless litany of terrifying choices that shredded her soul. A father's alcoholism. A brother's suicide. A mother's incessant marital unfaithfulness. Things that I could never have comprehended. Hers was a devastated life beyond description: a human holocaust.

And it all poured into the night, across the rock and timber altar, down the gravel floor, out into the deep woods, and into the expanses of heaven itself. When it was done, she was free and her core was cleansed. Likewise, I was free. In that chapel, God gave me far more than I had ever expected as I had trod the dirt and gravel path earlier that night. I saw bits of me in her, and they were likewise swept away in her release.

The next sunrise may have actually been her very first sunrise, the day dawning over a new life. With the sun barely warming the eastern horizon, she went to the shower. Her clothes were deposited in the washer. She combed her hair into long translucent waves, brushed her teeth bright, and put on fresh, clean clothes. A touch of borrowed make-up and a sprits of perfume rounded out the transformation. Arranging herself in the mirror, she gently primped herself to perfection.

She walked into the cafeteria for that final breakfast wholly new. Silence fell over 100 campers. Its power was deafening. With all our superficial judgments, we defined her. So complete were those judgments we all sat there trying to make them fit this new person for, sadly, we knew no other way to define her. The old judgments of a monster melted away in the light of their gross insufficiency and a fresh understanding of this remarkable young woman seized the room. A litany of miracles walked in with her.

At that final breakfast, she went from table to table to table. Asking for forgiveness from those she'd hurt. Weeping with those whose lives she'd scarred. Holding the faces of so many in her hands, looking intently into their eyes and telling them how sorry she was. Hugging and holding and crying with an endless array of campers and counselors. No one ate breakfast that morning because sometimes life becomes bigger than food and larger than any agenda. Sometimes life intersects us so powerfully the only thing we can give attention to is that which intersects us. And Susan intersected us all.

A revival broke out in that cafeteria. Clusters of young lives gave themselves to God over eggs, bacon and a radically changed life. Busses and arriving cars were asked to wait until the surge of one life changed had fully raced and run through the dozens of other hurting lives that morning. The vast gulf between what we were and what we could be was searingly highlighted in Susan. And in the end, God ravaged the work of Satan and the deep pain of innumerable adolescents through the life of a single young lady who chose to see her core and live differently because of it. It was the most remarkable thing I have ever seen: a wretched and putrid life, detested by those around her, changing the very lives of those who had hated her, thereby, leaving a legacy of life.

An Errant Judgment
The rocks had dropped one by one. Each thud stirred a slight wisp of dust that quickly settled, and with it, a slight wisp of hope, of life. Garbled whispering rose from the gathered cluster of religious leaders. Cutting glances rendered razor sharp with hatred were slung across the courtyard. Righteous indignation wrapped itself, like a robe, around pious bodies. And then, there was a slow dispersing of those gathered in their robes and finery, the oldest leaving first. The sound of feet on departing gravel built and then lessened as the courtyard emptied. Soon silence drifted in, leaving the scene still with lifeless rocks that attested to hatred halted and judgment deferred. All that was left was a prostitute and the Son of God; someone less than human groveling in the guilt of promiscuity – and Jesus. Hollowness and Wholeness. One on one.

Half naked, the hours had been truncated with deception, discovery, detainment and deliberation. Deep in an illicit sexual embrace, eyes were watching, peering past slightly parted curtains. A door stood ajar. Shooing away curious passersby, and under the guise of righteous action, they collected visual evidence as to the unfolding offense while hiding the feeding of their own sensate passion by vicariously engaging in the heat of passion themselves. The trap was sprung. She was seized; a few loose garments were thrown around her naked body; heckles of debauchery were hurled; and she was dragged away. Her partner somehow vanished, as his purpose was fulfilled.

Jesus stood slowly. His eyes, contemplative, shifted from the marks scrawled in the dirt and drew across the empty courtyard. It is painful that people condemn in others that which they cannot accept in themselves, that somehow the act of condemning it in others supposedly frees them from the very same thing. They have, in some way, proven themselves invincible to whatever they are confronting because they have identified it and confronted it in another. In doing so, they somehow view themselves as insulated from that same thing. Judging is most often not a necessary action, but an action rooted in the fear of those initiating the action. It is a self-centered action designed to free the one judging from the belief that they will ever be consumed or controlled by that which they are judging. The boldness of love had succumbed to the fear of self and the narcissism of self-preservation manifested in their judgment of this woman. The rocks that littered the courtyard yelled it loudly.

He drew a slight breath, paused, and then turned. Before Him there knelt a hollow human being. Few turn to her profession unless there is scathing emptiness. There are few people in life who are so relentlessly hollow and hold a relentless self-hatred. She had likely arrived at that moment hollow and empty, in desperate need of a touch, an affirmation. Receiving even a morsel of someone's heart and life might have been just enough to pull her up and out of the life she had lived. Empathy instead of judgment; compassion instead of condemnation; love instead of legalism; someone who might look beyond the putrid exterior to see the person inside.

Men had used her, violating her for a few coins. Seeing her only as an object upon which to release their sexual tensions and live out their distorted fantasies, they had been unwilling to see the person who died a little more after each illicit rendezvous. Not caring to see. Judging, but judging differently. Judging how she might be used by them and attempting to determine what assets they could abduct in the vandalism of another human being.

Then there was the disgust of other men thrown out in taunts and heckling as she made her way through tight streets. Vendors refused to sell her goods. Still other men wanted to stone her, to kill her, to rid the world of her without understanding why she was who she was. All of them rendered their sordid judgments, each colored by their place of proximity and point of orientation to her life. This was the same thing I had done to Susan.

Yet here was a different kind of man. He is the kind of man I would like to be. His example both prompts and prods me to grapple with my inadequacies that I might do the same as He did. Jesus had no need to judge. He did not need to judge her to feel insulated against her atrocities. He had no need to elevate Himself over her to feel safe from that which had destroyed her. He was not concerned with advancing Himself or His interests at her expense.

He stood in the breech and turned the condemnation away. 'Woman, where are they? Has no one condemned you?' (John 8:10 NIV) The voice of condemnation was suddenly still and hauntingly absent. She was free of the condemnation that had overwhelmed her life. It was an odd and alien experience. She was no longer suppressed by the judgments of others designed to elevate themselves. She was not sacrificed out of the need of someone else to feel superior. She was free to be different and to do different.

Often God intervenes in ways that are outside our realm of experience. The very thing we need, we cannot conceptualize. But it is these very things Jesus brings to us. And in the perfect freedom of the moment, we are frozen. Likewise, she was unable to look up. The silence made it clear. This man had turned away the wrath that had followed her all her life. The stones of judgment lay still in the dust. Their voice had been muted. Caught in the void, she attempted to somehow acclimate to it. She floundered in the freedom where judgment was absent. She was free to be who she truly was without the proclaimed judgments of others forcing her to remain who she had been. She stammered with the words forming in the midst of mental groping and said, 'No one, sir' (John 8:11 NIV). It was just the two of them. She was face to face with this man, alone in the courtyard of her life.

Our Courtyards
'Then neither do I condemn you … Go now and leave your life of sin' (John 8:11 NIV). It was not about judgment or punishment. There was no recitation of sins, no lengthy exposé on the spiritual and psychological implications of sexual sin. There was no need. It was clear. It was known. Her choices were not the point of discourse, for they were only the manifestation of pain, not the pain itself. The lacerated core bludgeoned by so many others was what defined her. It was not outward appearances or the manifestation of behaviors, not her acts of sexual promiscuity, but

the terrified and bloodied inner self that repulsed others so that it would not incur further damage. She sought to protect herself against the loss of any more blood of emotion. One must refuse to judge as judgment only sentences those who judge to that which they judge in others. Rather, we must take a different tact and attempt to see past the behavior to the person behind the behavior.

Likewise, I have stood in many of my life's own courtyards. There, in those places, inherent in me, is the fundamental knowledge regarding my own nature and the manifest actions of that nature. I often pretend that is not the case, rummaging forward through the accumulated filth of my life, pretending not to know the reason for its accumulation. Playing dumb. Feigning ignorance. Judging others ruthlessly so that I think myself superior and insulated from being what they are, thereby, escaping accountability. But I know. I know full well.

But those who condemn me have departed. The rightful punishment is suspended. Justice as I perceive it has been placated and postponed. All that should be happening to me is not. And in the absence of judgment is freedom. God renders all judgment void because of the cross. The distractions, demands and declarations of the world as it rails against my sin are silent. They are gone, unable to shackle me to my sin through judgment of it. Everything that would give me pause to defend defenseless actions is absent, for there is no judgment against which I must defend myself. Every voice that would legitimately describe the repercussions of my behaviors has fallen silent. Justice is suspended in silence. And it is only God. My sin and God. The freedom to be different.

A Choice Freed from Judgment
What was her choice? After He turned and left, she stood there, aghast and paralyzed. With the sunrise, an entirely new day would dawn for her. In the months and years ahead, she would wash Jesus' feet with her tears. She would attend to Him; push through the crowds that hailed Him and then condemned Him; follow Him through the pressing mobs and winding streets of Jerusalem to Golgotha. She would endure those three and a half hours on the cross that seemed an eternity. She would watch Him die; wait through that Saturday with angst indescribable; and be the first to see Him risen. Her life would be radically new in ways incomprehensible to her, being wrenched out of the bed of prostitution and propelled to partnership

with the Messiah. All because Someone refused to bind her with His judgments and instead, sought her freedom.

The End Product

The bus had rumbled up the long gravel road of the camp, dust and diesel leaving a path attesting to its journey, the wake dissipating and thinning in a slight summer breeze. Clusters of birds raised a cacophony of song in the dense foliage of the surrounding woods. Golden sunshine rained from a generous sky of blue. Hundreds of sunburned campers with suitcases, duffle bags and rich memories gathered in clusters around a myriad of cars, busses and vans that inundated the parking lot. In the departing mayhem, there was a tug on my shoulder. A transformed face greeted me. This was not the girl who came off this same bus six days earlier. Instantly I was in the grip of a hug dripping with the love of a grateful heart. Long and rich. The hug of life and living. In the midst of the embrace, she whispered, Thanks so much. I'll never be the same again.

Her bus rolled off down that driveway, leaving a trail of dust and diesel as it had when it arrived. On board was a miracle. God had gotten to the core of her courtyard and suspended judgment. There she seized the second chance. And it changed her forever.

Pondering Point

We judge based on externals. It is easy that way. There is no expenditure of energy attempting to ascertain that which we cannot see. Seizing and evaluating the obvious is easy. It allows us to render rapid judgment and avoid encountering life at its core. It is cheap living that is superficial and thin. We do the same with ourselves. We are distant from our own cores. That, however, is where Jesus meets us. Here we are afforded two things: genuine repentance centered in the acknowledgment of our core and the chance to do something radically different, a wild departure into the fullness of life and the fullness of God.

A Thought
- Am I willing to see myself at my very core, with the absence of appearances and fronts?
- Will I dare that kind of honesty, being aware of what I lose?
- Am I willing to respond to that revelation by choosing a radically different course for my life, one that may touch the entirety of my

life?

Chapter 7
The Pool

I caught it out of the corner of my eye, nearly missing it except for an accidental glance. It was something bursting onto the stage of life in silent subtlety. It handed a precious moment to those with eyes keen enough, or lucky enough, to see past the mayhem of living to the miracle set as a bejeweled stone in the gold setting of life. Slight and unobtrusive, it unfolded before me. My mind analyzed it sterile until my heart wrenched it away and made it soft, the tender threads of a magnificently marred tapestry.

It was a short distance – for healthy legs, but a vast expanse for tiny, useless appendages. He was dressed for church as would be any six-year-old boy, a dress shirt giving him an air of pending adulthood yet years away. Black dress shoes were scuffed at the toes and sides. A shiny black belt girded navy blue dress pants that were slightly worn at both knees. His frame was tiny and slight, suggesting both a fragile body and a fragile heart. On his knees, peering out the double glass door at the front of the church, he sat, a small parking lot and a patch of grass away. Longing and foreboding were swirling through a six-year-old heart whose legs were unresponsive in delivering him to that for which he longed.

The object of his attention was our dog. All 98 pounds of love, licks and affection sat in our front yard. She was a furry invitation to love and be loved. His tender heart yearned to come and play. Spina bifada refused to let his legs carry him there. They refused to carry him anywhere, rendering them limp appendages that had forsaken their role and robbed a little boy of his boyhood. And so Dustin sat yearning behind a double glass door until the yearning was too much. It was then I caught it. I will never forget.

A fragile six-year-old frame filled with passion to love and be loved made him drag unresponsive legs across the parking lot. Atrophied, they trailed behind him as useless appendages that would just as soon not take this journey. Planting thin arms in front of himself, he drew his tiny body ahead a few precarious inches. Again, putting palms to concrete, he would lift his torso and slide forward yet another few inches. His eyes were fixed on the dog. Determination was etched across a young brow. Lips were pursed and tight in the throes of physical exertion. Persistent. Defiant. The few who witnessed the monumental effort found themselves stymied in admiration, ashamed at the fragility of their own efforts at life and living.

It was a manifestation of the desperation of a young life to live despite the handicap that threw an insurmountable barrier across his path. He was ever resistant, forcing himself into life in lieu of the resources that would have naturally taken him there, refusing to be relegated to the fringes of society and the sparse borderlands of living. But he was six, the number of his surgeries the same. And yet he remained ecstatically alive, infused with all the energy of a little boy, yet lacking the legs to seize that energy and race off into life. It all struck me as he set out to drag himself to us, a small parking lot and a patch of grass away. But it is not always that way. I watched him, fearing he might eventually succumb to the hopelessness that enshrouds so many; relegating themselves to the very borderlands that he, by virtue of his efforts at that precise moment, was trying to avoid. Refusing to be beaten, he dragged himself forward. And then, another thought: *His handicap is evident. Mine, which are just as inhibiting, are hidden, but they are just as devastating.*

How Large a Small Distance
The clamor could be heard rising from the temple complex. It spilled over the temple wall: waves of jubilation, bleating of sheep, lowing of cattle, chants of ancient hymns, squeals of running children, cooing of doves from lofty marbled precipices – all lapping the distant hills. The jostling of the masses in worship and celebration could also be heard. The rotund bellow of the ram's horn sent a deep summons, its thick call washing over the wall and rolling out into the countryside. It quickly became thin as a vapor of sound, eventually dispelling on rolling hills and deep into lonely olive groves. Smoke rose, drifted and floated, becoming diluted into ever

thinning wisps by a passive breeze. A thin haze hung over the temple, slowly dissipating at its own edges.

On the road south from Jericho, there was a continual flow of the faithful. Caravans were weighed with provisions. Flocks of sheep pressed tightly in a woolen flow, coursing toward the Sheep Gate, portents of the sacrifices to be made. Cages burst with the wild fluttering of confined wings. There was the velvet cooing of doves. Lumbering cattle lazily grazed on sporadic clumps of grass, the tight snap of leather whips being only a minor irritant. Muscular flanks of oxen were tight and lean. Sturdy hooves pounded the ground, drawing carts loaded high with supplies and goods. Already hawking their wares, sellers worked the arriving crowd. Broad gestures proclaiming the value of the product added a hint of drama. Here was the once-in-a-lifetime deal being offered with the flagrant passion of a mesmerizing charlatan. And for days, this was the scene along the road.

But he was not part of it. For 38 years, he had not been part of it. He watched it come and go from a distant place of immobility and isolation. His mind unencumbered, he had sent it there to walk the streets, smell the smoky sweet aroma of the sacrifices, gaze up at the smooth marbled walls that challenged the sky for supremacy and mingled with the throbbing crowd. He stood there as the ram's horn bellowed fat and deep, sending pigeons bursting into the sky and the massive crowd below into a reverent silence. Prayers were murmured. Psalms were uttered in ancient chants. The weak eyes of the old were cast upward, and the fresh eyes of the young strained to understand. He was at peace, but only momentarily.

North of the temple wall lay the pool of Bethesda. It was little more than a stone's throw away, though, in reality, it was a world away. It was brimming with the collective accumulation of defective humanity. They were sequestered and tucked away, thereby, whitewashing the face of the culture by putting the less desirable elements out of view. They were relegated to the borderlands of life. Here the human wreckage coalesced and mingled, wallowing in the depravity of their condition. The collective sound of the festival filtered through the colonnades just enough to remind the outcasts of the world they were not part of. Weakened by the distance that divided the two worlds, the myriad sounds drifted diminished over the pool. Yet there was nothing festive there, only the taunting reminder of how large a small distance can be when one is handicapped. Here there was only pain, suffering and deep hopelessness.

Why Jesus went to the pool, we do not know. Scripture leaves His decision for the stuff of conjecture. But it was likely that love drew Him. He was God walking among the wounded and finding a home among the handicapped. And so, He went. The mood, the atmosphere and the tenor at the pool held no trace of the festivities. The sounds of merriment and celebration that drifted overhead found no correlation there. They were otherworldly. Celebration was absent – utterly so, providing a stunning contrast. Jesus stepped through the colonnades and paused, drinking in the scene of human wreckage strewn around the pool. The depravity washed away any festive notion. All hints of gaiety vanished. Celebration evaporated. God was in the carnage, not in the celebration, choosing instead to walk among the filth, not the festivities. He was not in the drama, but in the dregs. He was not at the portico; He was at the pool.

The Handicaps
He skirted the colonnades and watched, peering across the vestiges of discarded humanity. Cavernous sockets both dark and deep reached out for light and found none. Eyelids edged with a crusty film attempted to trace sound and probe silence, following voices with canted heads. Without sight and catching only shards of sound, they pieced them together in an attempt to apprehend the world, creating a mosaic of the clamor and clatter of the world painted across blind minds. But it was no substitute. Yearning for what you cannot see brings no sight. Hope is held to exhaustion where it can be held no longer, forcing the blind to die desperately desiring what they cannot comprehend. And so they clustered around the pool — and they waited.

Theirs were palsied limbs: truncated, stubby and atrophied. Their joints protruded in gangly knobs of bone tightly covered in weathered skin. Appendages lay twisted in gross contortions that had a ghastly aura about them. Crawling and grasping, they attempted to embrace some semblance of living with a debilitating handicap; they lay weighed down with the terrible shame over which they had no control. Their minds were desirous of living, but their bodies callously refused that wish. And so they clustered around the pool – and they waited.

Paralysis befalls a body that refuses to respond to the commands of the mind, being entirely unsympathetic to the hope of the heart. The clarity, the distinction of the mind as separate from the body is no clearer than here, in these lives strewn around the colonnades. Milky white salvia traced thin lines down assorted chins and dripped off beards. Sopping clothing was bathed in mucous. Words were slurred and, at times, incomprehensible. They lay drawn up in atrophied bundles of twisted flesh, littered throughout the colonnades. It was the barest existence. And so they clustered around the pool – and they waited.

The colonnades cut the morning sun, carving long shadows that threw themselves across the court and dipped into the murky green waters of the pool. Moans of discomfort arose in a sporadic chorus of pain and babbling incoherence that gave full voice to the futility of their conditions. Cries of pain rose and then drew down into silence. Birds flitted among the structures, oblivious to the wreckage below. Their songs were somehow misplaced, being very much out of sorts there. And this Jesus scanned the pool.

Jesus at Our Pools
There was profound poignancy to one. The severity of his condition was deepened by duration. "... he had been in this condition for a long time" (John 5:6 NIV), paralysis enfolding in upon itself time and time again. Multiplied misery was increasingly layered upon itself, being terribly punctuated and made stale with time. Jesus knelt beside him and scanned the fleshly wreckage, drawing in each imperfection and every distortion of what this man was created to be. Brushing away the circling flies in a gentle sweeping motion, He pulled a tattered garment over an exposed shoulder, ran gentle fingers down a twisted trunk, then tenderly cupped an atrophied head in a broad hand. Forcing this collision of man and God, He directed His stare into the man's weary eyes and forcefully voiced the greatest question — the only question: "Do you want to get well?" (John 5:6 NIV)

The perfect invitation was extended, prompted entirely without a request; the question was directed to one in dire need of the question. However, the contemplation of healing had been so long in duration that the paralytic's mind was reduced to a single possibility, one option, one way to be healed. And this had become his focus for 38 years. His mind, like his body, was in paralysis, but of a different sort. I have no one to help me into the pool when the water is stirred (John 5:7 NIV).

Myopic Vision and My Plan
Gross tunnel vision: I have it, I live in it, and I respond to my world out of it. God is welcome to intersect my life. In fact, He is passionately invited to do so. But I relegate His work to a box, forcing Him to function within the tightly finite parameters of my thinking, which have evolved entirely within the limits of my handicaps. There is no room for the miraculous. Instead, I attempt to calculate how the impossible might transpire, trying to outline the footsteps of the Infinite before He shows up. When God comes, I have the obvious solution ready for Him. I think I possess the only real possibility that effectively addresses my need, my handicap. And I am brash enough in my ignorance to instruct God.

There is no surrender in this. I have already predetermined the path to my healing and determined what it will take. I have decided the course of action that is necessary. All God needs to do is implement what I have already ascertained as bringing healing in my life. Am I blind? Or am I ignorant? Am I brash? Do I deem myself so acquainted with my handicap that this familiarity has given me the expertise to devise the solution? It would seem to be a mix of it all. God does not bring the miraculous into my life. He simply provides the vehicle to get to my predetermined destination. A push into the pool is all I need. It is terribly rudimentary at best. God is demoted to some sort of menial assistant.

The Futility of Our Plans
It was not to be. The man would never dip himself in the pool. His healing did not lie in those waters. It was much simpler than that. There was no need for something external such as the waters of a pool. It was not about the inclusion of some element that God had to incorporate in order to bring about his healing. It was not about a plan; mythology; the utilization of an array of finite resources; the establishment of an effective strategy; or all the combined mental fortitude of man. It was about encountering God – one on one, as simple as it is powerful.

Jesus' voice was calm but sure. "Get up! Pick up your mat and walk" (John 5:8 NIV). Thirty-eight years of disability vanished in the span of eight simple words. Limbs instantaneously became firm and straight. Atrophied muscle was suddenly ripped strong. Misshapen joints were drawn and twisted perfect. A wholly unfamiliar vitality rose through his trunk and leapt out through his limbs, warming and igniting every tendon and every shred of muscle. And then he stood — for the first time in 38 abysmal years. Overwhelmed by the alien nature of the experience, he found himself doing that for which he dreamt a thousand times and more. Eyes gaped in disbelief. A tentative step, followed by another and yet another, engulfed him in the wonder of walking. Confidence mounted with each step until he was dancing, spinning and leaping. He stood wonderfully aghast, unable to absorb the remotest sense of what had happened.

He paused, knelt on new legs, and tenderly picked up his mat, folding it into rolls of reflection. He stood and scanned the pool, slowly realizing that was no longer where he belonged. In an instant, his life had been dislocated and relocated. Turning to Jesus, who had drawn back and watched the manifestation of life restored, he uttered a simple thank you crammed full with 38 years of incalculable pain. Setting out, he walked past a column, running a contemplative hand across its cool marbled surface. One final glance back at almost four decades of his life, and he walked out of the colonnades into the city, leaving behind a pool he never needed.

His Prescription for My Paralysis
How foolish I am to write my own prescription. I look to pools I never needed, so enamored with myself that I should think to know the course to my own healing. So often I am so foolish. I am grateful God does not often attend to my methodologies. His love shapes His directness, and I am so grateful He is direct. Slipping into my own sense of self-sufficiency, I am less than fully submitted to God. And here I am in danger from my own devices and my fabricated solutions. At these places, I need God to step in and say, "Take up your mat," whatever my mat is, and there are many of them. He must level me with His directness, bypassing all my constructs, all the pools I think so necessary, and thrust me to the healing I so desperately need. I must get out of my own way – and out of His. Forget the pool. Just get up and walk! For this, I praise Him and love Him.

Dustin's Victory
And then, he was there, having navigated the small parking lot and that patch of lonely grass, dragging those useless appendages that would demand he not live. A crowd of observers had watched it unfold, seeing in him the tenacity of a young heart unwilling to let a handicap dictate his

life. Caught up in the wonder and love of my 98-pound dog, they melded into one another. Held in the furry embrace of love and licks, he said, "God don't want me to live by my handicap! He helped me crawl right over here." He did not have a preconceived idea of what God needed to do in his life. He was not consumed by his own conceptualizations of how God should intersect His handicap. He did not sit on the fringes of life and yearn for more. He was open to whatever God was going to do at whatever moment He was going to do it. At that moment, he took up his mat and walked. So must I.

Pondering Point
We all have our handicaps: some apparent, some not. But we have them. And in some way, they relegate us to the pools in life, the fringes and borderlands of life and living. Here we apply our own solutions. In time, their inadequacy fails us and we succumb. Having succumbed to them, we stay in those places, those places that are only a small parking lot and a patch of grass away from real living.

A Thought
- What are my handicaps?
- How have I attempted to solve them?
- Am I ready to admit that my plans have failed? And am I ready to allow God to apply the right prescription?

Chapter 8

I Am That One: Sheep in the Cesspool

Today it was a transient, a chance passing as I walked my dog. Ashamedly, I tried to avoid him as he staggered down the street in erratic steps laced with the staleness of alcohol. He drew up his weathered pack, shifted its weight and limped toward me. The concourse of my mind coursing with presumed pleas for money, or a scattered discourse of his misfortunes, or any number of sordid stories or pleas I simply didn't want to hear. But he wanted to pet my dog. That's all. It was an agenda of love and loneliness that might somehow be carried out by petting my dog, nothing more.

Bedraggled, his skin was weathered thick and dark. Deep creases were packed with sweaty grime. Hair, oily, stringy and wild, exploded in tangles from the edges of a perspiration stained baseball cap. A beard, patchy and streaked with gray before its time, incompletely littered his face. Filth was layered deep into polyester pants and turned a white t-shirt shades of sweaty brown. The stitching was frayed on the fringes of tennis shoes worn thin by the road of wandering. His fingernails were embedded with the dirt of desperation, clawing life's sparse soil for a morsel of sustenance. His teeth were rotted and black from years of inattention. And he wanted to pet my dog.

My first response was one of revulsion. My second – suspicion about his intent.

"What's her name?" he asked.

A small connection was established. I moved toward him and let out the leash. His eyes were filled with loneliness, the starvation of human isolation.

"Aspen," I said. "She loves people."

He dropped his aged pack, knelt, put his hands on both sides of her face and said, "You're a pretty girl."

Then, with uncharacteristic compassion he hugged her, wrapping his arms around her 98-pound body and holding her close. Both melded into each other for a moment, meeting a need in the life of the other. Innocence and acceptance merged, paving the way for intimacy free of risk and completely open to vulnerability. They did something I rarely see or do myself. They genuinely connected in something so pure and undiluted that days of contemplation left me with but the barest understanding of what had transpired. For a brief moment, the disheveled man was alive – vibrantly alive. And in his aliveness, I saw my deadness.

A moment passed. Then stiffly he drew himself to his feet and said, "She's lucky to have you."

He then paused and nodded to himself, absorbing the moment so as to be able to draw from it in any one of the innumerable lonely moments that were yet to be his. Then he drew up sagging pants, shouldered his pack, said thanks and lumbered away. He turned the corner, and I never saw him again.

I stood in the middle of the road in a deluge of shame, caught in the swirling stench of my judgmental attitude and putrid sense of superiority, understanding that I was no different than the man who had only moments earlier turned and walked out of my life. I was him. In that encounter, I was far less than him. Impatient with my introspection, the dog pulled the leash, jostling me from my thoughts. I cinched the leash in my hand and resumed our walk. Focused with soulful scrutiny on the corner the man had rounded, my mind wandered.

Sheep in the Cesspool
The muck and manure of society. Swirling sewage collected, running

down the gutter of the culture. It was repelling. People are associated as one with their behaviors; their actions are seen as defining their character and declaring their worth, these things stating their value. They were irrevocably tied to, branded by and labeled within their actions, viewed as lost, unsalvageable and obviously irretrievable. The excrement of all that is evil and decadent swirled in a morbid societal stew. They were tax collectors, prostitutes, assorted thieves and drunkards. All were drawn deep from the dregs of society. It was the cesspool of the culture, and in the middle of it all, Jesus stood knee deep. Holiness in filth. God in the cesspool. It was implausible – but there He was.

Others of a different sort also scanned the crowd that day. They visually infiltrated the many gathered in tight clusters to hear Him. The decadence was clear to pharisaical eyes and those narrowed by the law. She wore the vestiges of a prostitute. She had been seen in closed, muted conversation with various men on street corners and deep in alleys. Currency had been exchanged. It was followed by covert slippage into nearby residences. Lustful embraces. Eroticism was exchanged for cash. There she was. And there He was.

Stretching pious necks, they scanned the crowd further. There they stood, having been seen at their tables far too often – garnering inflated taxes. They gouged the lives and harvested the purses of kindred and neighbors. They grew interminably fat on the sweat of others and showered themselves with the dividends of lives stolen and hopes exonerated. They lived lavishly, sucking as itinerant leeches of an oppressive ruling nation. Garnished in costly robes, faces soft, hands smoothed, and skin scented with the stolen privileges of luxury, they sported both gold and silver decor. There they were. And there He was.

Eyes scanned the crowd further. There, next to several others, stood another. Aged by alcohol, there were those who remained unsteady even when sober. The stench of stale liquor and vomit exuded a putrid aroma all around them. They were a host of slaves to a liquid escape that had drawn their families, their reputations, their money, and their lives down to the dregs. The sum total of their existence had been drowned in a bottomless drink, subsisting solely on the hope of the next drink. There they were. And there He was.

Others gathered, mingled and drew close to Him. The poor. Widows. Those marked with the physical handicaps that bespeak the gravity of their presumed sins. The diseased and deformed mingled about, each a walking testament to their transgressions and to God's judgment. An assortment of sin pooled in one place, it was a living, breathing cesspool of everything that makes humanity pathetic. It was a vortex of all that is unrighteous, distilled in one location. Wretched were they all. And there He stood. It was incomprehensible.

The feelings were stated and the behavior condemned. "This man welcomes sinners and eats with them" (Luke 15:2 NIV). Do I think any differently? Really? I think not. Of course I rail against the audacity of their comments, but inwardly, my heart is theirs. Why? Because I don't see myself in the crowd. I observe such as these, but from a distance, detached and somehow better, not having succumbed as they had. Possessing some inflated sense of worth that insulates me from my own humanity, I think I am a different sort of person, as if there are degrees of humanity. I judge them all on abhorrently false premises, just like I did the transient. Thoughts of pompous superiority keep me different from them, thoughts that are preposterous because I am there in the cesspool, too. I am just the same. I am one of them. I'm no better – maybe worse. All I am is as much a part of the cesspool as any of them. And that is why He loves me. That is why He incessantly looks for me and chases me.

Jesus paused and realized that those who presume righteousness are in greater need than those who recognize their decadence. He understood the orientation of those who condemned His actions, those who could not comprehend God in the cesspool. He raised His voice and projected it farther, drawing in His detractors by intonation. "Suppose one of you has a hundred sheep and loses one of them. Does he not leave the ninety-nine in the open country and go after the lost sheep until he finds it?" (Luke 15:4 NIV) It's about God in a mad search for the one; a desperate pursuit of the solitary soul; on a divine manhunt of love for His creation. His is a heart too big to miss even one life hopelessly lost in the tangled wilderness of living. Out in the wilds of life, the loss of the one outweighs the safety of the many. So much so the cesspool is a must. Unrelenting. Unstoppable. He has to be there.

And so, He was standing in the midst of lost sheep, in the path of life of those who had wandered. Some had wandered far. Many were in grave danger. None were able to find their way back. Each was lost — unless the Shepherd sought them; searched for them; scratched through the caustic dust to find traces of them. He scoured the countryside and navigated treacherous paths. He descended steep cliffs and ascended rocky precipices, risking His life in order to retrieve theirs. He willingly gave His life to ensure their safe return. This journey, this search, would, in time, require His life for these gathered around Him. It required His life for me.

I am that lost sheep He comes in search of. I am he. I am them! It is a stunning revelation, relegating me to base authenticity. It strips the accumulated layers that provide me a pretence not my own. Feigning what I am not and subsequently forgetting who I am, I am lost in a deluge of personal aggrandizement that is paper thin. In time, I import the lie so effectively I have fooled myself and marred who God made me. And a simple transient, bedecked with his authenticity, exposed me.

When I fully embrace that I am the transient and that I am all the people who were with Jesus in that place, my acknowledged depravity forces me to ask, "What then is lost in my loss?" Am I, in the vast expanse of creation, covered with the filth of my depravity, of that much importance? With my disobedience; my bumbling; my foolish decisions and defiant behaviors; my judgmental attitude that betrays the whole of it all; and my innate presumption of superiority – am I worth the cost of seeking me out and finding me?

And then, too often, I am embarrassed to be found. My depravity is vividly exposed in the finding. Shame is given terrifying release and horrendously devastating power when laid bare before others. Accountability is demanded that I can forgo in isolation. It is safer to be lost. And so not only am I lost — I hide. Drawn, sick and disgusted by my disobedience, I am unworthy of the search and wholly unworthy of discovery. But search He does, and He does so relentlessly. He pursues me, overcoming every obstacle in His mad quest to redeem me yet again. There is a divine wildness in His persistence to ferret me out and bring me home. And for this, among many other things, I love Him desperately. I fear Him finding me, but I am desperate to be found. And find me He does.

And then a final caveat. A glimpse of what thrills heaven. Of what sends electric excitement through the halls of the infinite. "I tell you that in the same way there will be more rejoicing in heaven over one sinner who repents than over ninety-nine righteous persons who do not need to repent" (Luke 15:7 NIV). And so heaven cheers, raising a raucous shout of exhilaration when He finds me, when He found those gathered around Him that day. A compassion breaks and surges in a tidal wave of exuberant joy. The foundations of heaven shake. Angels break in thunderous applause. Waves course through the concourses of the infinite, shake the pillars of the universe, and rumble off to the edges of eternity. How terrible to be lost. How magnificent to be found!

The prostitute succumbed, repented and prostrated her life. Heaven cheered, angels applauded. Tax collectors bowed in abject remorse, faced with the skewed priorities that flew in the face of all that was good. The infinite was deluged. The drunkard sought living water instead of alcoholic inebriation, creating room to restore all that he had lost. The pillars of the universe were rocked. The blind, lame, diseased and those with assorted maladies – spiritual, emotional and physical – were found, and a shout of thunderous joy rumbled off to the fringes of space. It was unimaginable and grand beyond comprehension. I can only grasp a shred of it, sip but a drop. But that – even that – is exhilarating.

The religious and legal eyes of the others did not perceive it. The words of Jesus were direct. They painted a vivid picture. The clarity. The definition. The assorted hues, colors, shapes, dramas and intrigue were all apparent. But their correlation was not possible for pharisaical eyes. Sheep and a cesspool of dredged humanity did not resonate nor correlate. A cesspool was all they saw. It was all they could see, nothing more. All the while, heaven was wildly boisterous with the thunder of lost sheep now found. I had pharisaical eyes that day. I saw the cesspool. I did not see the sheep — even when the sheep was right in front of me, petting my dog and talking to me. It doesn't get any closer than that, and I missed it entirely. I am ashamed.

All I See is Cesspool
I miss it, too, in my own life and in the lives around me. I miss the magnitude of my own deprivation and the degree of lostness to which it speaks and the love of God for me that relentlessly drives His wild and unrelenting search to find me. The contrast between the two is so broad,

so massive. The meeting of the two is so obviously thunderous. How can such an event over me be so profound? How can others — the filthy, the walking wounded, the degenerate, the self-centered, the calloused – so much like me – be of such import? How can these – how can we – be so valuable, so precious, that heaven itself raises the roof of the cosmos in applause?

I don't understand it. I work to believe it. And I am profoundly appreciative for it. I want to see myself as terribly fallen as everyone else – and as worthy as He sees me. I want to see others in the same way. I want His eyes. I want to see my filth as simply a lost sheep among many lost sheep, a lost sheep He is passionately searching for with an infinite aggression. And when I pause and contemplate the wonder of it all, I am filled. I swell with His love. I am saturated with a profound sense of inestimable worth and count myself lucky to be amidst the human cesspool that God loves so dearly.

My pace quickened to round the corner and see if I might catch a glimpse of the transient. I turned and he was gone. Off to some unknown destination. His frayed shoes and gentle heart plodding the road of life. I paused for a lingering moment and shouted *thank you* down the empty street. My voice dissipated, likely unable to reach the man. I took one more glance down the empty road, longing to see the one who had helped me see. I turned and headed home, my heart thanking him for letting me see who I am and how great God is.

Pondering Point

Too often it's not that we can't see our depravity. For most of us, it is readily apparent. Our deficits and failures suffocate us. They are monsters that seize our lives and stifle any hope or promise of living. We are sheep imprisoned in failure, self-hatred, an overwhelming sense of incompetence, inferiority, the scars of horrific histories resulting in putrid self-disgust. More often than not, it is not difficult to see ourselves in the cesspool. The problem is we can't visualize ourselves being any place else. We forget Jesus stands in the cesspool right next to us. And He calls each of us out of that place. As frightening or impossible as it may seem, God has come in to take us out – to take *you* out.

A Thought
- Am I willing to risk exposure and the possibility of success because of the exposure?
- Has the cesspool defined me and held me captive because of that definition?
- Am I willing to dare to believe that I am infinitely more than I have come to believe myself to be?

Chapter 9
Two Thin Ones

A single quarter and a lonely nickel lay in his palm, the sum a mere 30 cents, marginal and of little monetary value. His hands were gnarled, his tendons drawing fingers up in a claw-like grasp that somehow seemed both pathetic and fiendish at the same time. Emaciated, they seemed little more than skin tightly drawn over skeletal protrusions that might have been the creation of some artist set on a fiendish agenda. Two coins were precariously cradled in a violently spastic palm framed by morbid deformity. It was the stuff of cerebral palsy.

His body was a larger manifestation of his contorted hands. Gnarled and spastic, his limbs were atrophied thin, giving them the illusion of brittleness and fragility. Skin skirted slight sinews of sparse muscle and wrapped itself tightly around bony protrusions. A spinal cord was drawn irresistibly forward, having wrestled with gravity – and lost, rendering him a collapsed lump of humanity. Pencil thin legs were draped helplessly over metal footrests, two tremulous feet Velcroed into submission. A thin rivulet of mucous traced an errant line down a stubbly chin, eventually finding a path down a soaked shirt.

His voice was likewise muted by the gross contortions that rendered his vocal cords inoperable. He had been born into this condition, knowing nothing other than this skeletal and spastic depravity, forever shackled to a wheelchair by a terribly dysfunctional body. I stood before him somehow ashamed that I should be privileged to have a healthy body and that he did not. And in the midst of this mound of deformed humanity, he held out a quarter and a nickel.

I came to cherish Eddie over the years. No, I actually came to love him. He always wore a smile and extended a hand in friendship – always. He had a broken laugh, deeply marred by CP, but woven with the joy and wild laughter of heaven itself. Sometimes the best place to see perfection is deep within imperfection. His hope was relentless. Grieved by the pain in my life that I sometimes shared with him, he would lay an erratic hand on my arm, look up to heaven and then back at me and then toward heaven again. And then he would bow a bobbing head. Without words, he would pray for me. I never heard what he said. I didn't need to. Few have prayed so powerfully, so genuinely, and with such absolute conviction. The weakness of his body was more than made up for by the phenomenal strength of his spirit.

A tattered Bible stood watch at his bedside. I would affix his glasses to his face with a tight band around his head so the gross motor movements of his head and neck would not throw them to the floor. With me turning the pages for him, he would read for hours, saturating himself in God. Finding a favorite passage, he would laugh with the very joy of the angels themselves, so much so I often coveted the freedom that was neither touched nor diminished by his physical imprisonment. He was remarkable. And in his terribly spastic hand, he held out this quarter and this nickel.

"Thirty cents. For what?" I asked. Several bumbling guesses and I finally understood. He wanted me to give it to the church. It was 30 cents: a lonely quarter and a tarnished nickel that, once given, left his pockets entirely empty expect for lint and love. It was an offering of inestimable proportions. Everything within me said no because sometimes sacrifice like that is far too hard to watch. I don't have the strength to let another sacrifice like that because I don't have the strength to do it myself. So I told Eddie to keep it for something else. His commitment to sacrifice for his God overcame the limitations of his frame, and he nearly rose out of his wheelchair, waving the coinage in my face. I melted. Right there I watched sacrifice and commitment come together in a spastic life, and I was grieved because of my response to him.

I took the coins from his palm. He settled back into his chair. A contorted smile instantly threw itself from ear to ear as his irrepressible laugh filled the room and skipped down the hallway of the facility, reflective of the unfettered spirit from which it sprang. I told him I would see it got to the church.

What followed was one of those inexplicable moments. Heading out the door of the facility, I was taken with an irritating curiosity. Pausing in one of those life moments when we stop because something indefinable is crossing our path and seizing our spirit, I turned and went back to the office. Walking to the files, I pulled the patient accounts. Scrolling down, I came to Eddie's name and drew out a yellowed ledger. The balance on his account registered the balance of his heart: 30 cents. *The* 30 cents. They just didn't empty his pockets. They emptied everything. Suddenly the two coins became priceless. Instantly they weighed heavily in my hand, and they shook the core of my heart. I scooped up the ledger, seized the file, and returned to Eddie's room.

He knew. He knew before I walked in the door. He nodded and I knew. It was all he had. They were the sum total of his assets. And that was the source of his elation: the fact he had given himself in his entirety and had left nothing unto himself that would diminish what God does in a life when we abandon ourselves to Him. He laughed and motioned me out of his room. I knelt, placed my hand on a bony shoulder, looked into the deep eyes of faith set in a terribly deformed body and said, Eddie, you are a remarkable man. And he was.

A Temple and an Offering
Two coins – nearly paper thin. They were the smallest currency in circulation. A lepton is rightly translated thin one. They dropped; their weight so slight they barely made a sound; their value so insignificant they would make no difference to the cause for which they were given. They were immediately lost, engulfed in a mound of gold and silver coinage. She drew a thin wrap around herself, turned, and shuffled into obscurity. Setting a course of hopelessness, the compass of her life marked a bearing of destitution. But history had been made and a core truth heralded. She would never know she left the temple and walked into history.

Flocks of pigeons stirred. Bursting into flight, they were thrown against the sky. Circling, returning, approaching, wings beat the air to a halt as they lit on lofty marble precipices hundreds of feet above the sprawling courtyard. The Judean countryside rolled to the horizon and spilled off. A ram's horn, its bellow uneven, ancient and haunting, muscled its thick intonations toward the courtyard. Pigeons exploded, scattering yet again. Cascading down the temple wall, the call flooded the courtyard, bounced back, returned yet again, and breeched the marbled walls. It rolled deep and unabated, its surge gradually dissipating far out in the expanse of the Judean countryside.

Smoke rose and curled listlessly against the lucid blue sky. The scent of sacrifices drifted, distilling, and then dissipating into the clean morning air. The cattle bellowed softly. Erratic bleating of sheep set a more intrusive tempo. The velvet cooing of doves gave all a soft edge. An occasional wild fluttering of caged wings was reminiscent of the soul and sin, where one desires to soar and the other desires to shackle. Musty odors wafted through the soft air of a new day. Offal permeated the thick coats of animals destined for sacrifice. It was pungent at times. Hoofs, hollow and tentative, trod on cobbled surfaces, their sounds echoing off smooth marble stones, doubling the auditory experience. Long shadows wrapped cloaked arms around colonnades. Having spread across the courtyard, they found themselves in a gradual retreat in morning's advance.

An event was set to unfold in the Court of the Women. Thirteen collection boxes shaped as trumpets were set about. Adjacent to this place was the Gate Beautiful. Jesus sat against its cool marbled walls, the protracted arguments and residual tensions still reverberating through the colonnades of the Court of the Gentiles that sat on the other side of the gate. His authority had been questioned. A story of a vineyard, a rebuffed owner and condemnation shaped His response. Trick questions were thrown at Him -- Caesar's image, resurrection and marriage – casting a net to capture Him in the mire of their duplicity. The net had not been nearly big enough. More than that, it had been cast awkwardly. Yet the hardness of men in light of such a great gift continues to illustrate the fact that God is far too immense to be perceived by men unless God gives them the means to do so. Can it be true that men can see God and still not see God? They did, and He relocated to the Gate Beautiful. Disciples in tow milled about closely, yet equating following Jesus with euphoria and not yet having comprehended sacrifice as being unconditionally woven into that following. And it is likely He here first caught a glimpse of her. He saw in her that which was so woefully absent in His detractors – and is so fundamental to an authentic walk with God. He settled and watched. And then a principle unfolded, nearly undetected as is the manner in which most things of value unfold.

Who she was, where she came from, and the intricacies of her life are unrecorded and left for speculation. "All these others made offerings that they'll never miss ..." (Luke 21:4 The Message). Is that not the difference? Calculated giving that is weighed and measured against risk. Decisions designed to insulate from chance. Giving without substantive cost. An act of sacrifice absent of the very essence of sacrifice is no sacrifice. If my giving leaves something of myself, so that I am able to perpetuate a false sense of security, I limit what God can do through what I give. If I fit in this story of this unknown woman, it is here – right here.

I am everyone else that pushed past the widow that day. In the flurry of my life, I throw a few coins at God in the name of sacrifice. And then I am on to other demands. Hers is a faith, a focus that has eluded me. Hers is an abandonment that is total, that leaves nothing left for her to hold onto other than the faith that precipitated and prompted the act. It is a faith for which I thirst, for which I grasp and seize by only thin threads that snap too easily.

"She gave extravagantly what she couldn't afford – she gave her all!" (Luke 21:4 The Message) And so she set out that day. Thin. Gaunt. Her face was drawn, etched and furrowed. Tattered wraps were tightly drawn around a slight frame, frail from loss, the endless angst of life. Jagged lacerations cut deep flesh wounds across her soul. Her heart had been seared by the white hot heat of loss. She lived the crippling kind of woundedness that is left when life strikes in ways that defy the cry of explanation that might somehow soothe a soul. Her soul was bent by the weight of the unbearable. Tears came frequently. A trembling, feeble hand brushed them aside. She drew a breath, stiffened her resolve and set out.

She was intent on giving what she couldn't afford. Through winding streets, she pushed past cloisters of gathered people; drew aside for heavy pack animals; circumvented vendors hailing the proclaimed benefit of their wares. Two thin coins were held tightly in bony hands that seemed little more than skin tightly drawn over skeletal protrusions. Hers was a rush to sacrifice, knowing that any hope for her life lay there and there alone.

The market was not full of things she would like, but things she, in her desperation, needed. A few morsels of food to quell the sharp pangs of hunger. A sparse piece of weary fabric to better hold the cold at bay. A vile of pasty opaque ointment to sooth chapped skin. Two thin coins could purchase a bit of one of these. No, it would not be. She passed. Her steps were firm. The temple was in view, and God was in mind.

She was misplaced. Nothing of grandeur defined her. She stood in stark contrast to the majesty of the temple that surrounded her and raised itself boastfully into the Judean sky. It diminished and truncated her. It all made her smaller and of less import than she already was. For certain, she was brave. Some resolute thread ran through her soul and had tied a knot in her heart, sending a plumb line into the depths of God, taking her there to give out of the vast resources of impoverishment. The ram's horn bellowed again. The pigeons burst into flight. She found a place in line.

She was a widow, poor and likely alone. The lack of resources suggests no extended family. She was isolated, impoverished and destitute. Her earthly resources were tapped out and non-existent. And so she stood, meaningless and invisible to those around her. It was not recognized, even by her, that earthly impoverishment empties the vault of the soul to make room for the wealth of heaven. It was those around her who stood impoverished while she stood deep and dripping with eternal riches. It was all starkly visible to Jesus. It was irrelevant in the larger scheme of things, but terribly relevant to God. The majesty of the temple and the power of the rich appeared to render her as nothing. Flowing robes, lavish and richly ornamental. Gold rings set deep with precious stones. Silks and imported fabrics in ornate wraps abounded. The thick scent of costly spices and variant nards filled the air. Servants in attendance were dispatched on errands of importance. Positions of power awaited them – and lavish homes to which they would retire at day's end. In sharp contrast – two thin coins. Poverty and prosperity had been reversed. The line moved. She shuffled in cadence.

It is inherent in us to judge and to evaluate. Observing, we apply some standard and then draw conclusions based on our shallow sense of life and living. We rate, compartmentalize, ascribe value and apply labels. And so it was with this woman. Bedraggled, worn and threadbare, she moved in pensive and muted steps, holding two thin coins in brittle fingers. Her life is held in defining contrast to those around her in that line, in that society.

The same evaluation was apparently performed in the minds of the disciples. She had been labeled, and the nature of the label had caused them to move on, disregarding and discounting her. They didn't see anything in her other than what the world saw and thereby, missed the magnificence of the riches in the poverty. She reached the collection box, fingered the worn metal, and dropped in the coins. She paused; clasped weathered hands; uttered a brief prayer; turned and was gone for the rest of time. The moment was only seconds in duration, but its lessons are nothing less than eternal.

Jesus drew the disciples back to her; He reevaluated her; and then sent their worlds careening. He handed them different eyes that opened a radical vision. She was more than everything around her. What diminished her, she dwarfed; she towered over that which towered over her. She was the embodiment of God's heart, as was Eddie. It was a complete reversal so obvious the world missed it. The obvious was hidden in its own clarity. It was so easy to see that it was passed over, and therefore, became invisible because it was too visible. The temple and all that adorned it paled. But all of this did not find a place to settle, to root in the hearts of rural Galileans unfamiliar with such architectural splendor. Their eyes turned from the widow to the temple. "It will be thrown down," Jesus retorted (Luke 21:6 NIV). The story of the widow remained when the temple did not because one was of God, and the other was only a monument to a perception of Him.

The Suffocation of Calculation
I am calculated – sadly so. Calculation renders abandonment impossible. Calculation is control, pure and simple. It is balancing risk and the assessing of outcomes as a means of attempting to achieve safe sacrifice. This search for safe sacrifice, which is an oxymoron indeed, is one that is so calculated that I weigh the principle separate from the reality.

The essence of the principle is clear: that I abandon myself to God and incur whatever intentional risk in that abandonment. The principle's application to my life is lost in the consideration of how I can manage it safely. What was done that day, the profound nature of this single abandoned soul, is clear. I can speculate how to mirror that abandonment in my life and my actions. Theological and philosophical contemplations are easy. But bringing them home – into the heart of my actions and how I live my life – that is difficult. Playing the role in my head is flawless. Living the role in my heart – stumbling. Not being able to match the heart and actions of this women or Eddie is devastating. And I am disgusted with myself.

Whatever I hold is thin anyway, thin in that I hold it only for a moment. It is not eternal. It will not follow me. Therefore, holding it is useless. But more so, whatever I hold leaves just that much less room for heaven in my soul. Every nook and cranny of my life that is taken up with the stuff of this world leaves just that much less room for the stuff of eternity. God looks for vacancies as much as He is interested in orchestrating evictions. He searches and fills the space I have intentionally, of my own free will, made through the aggressive disposal of all the worldly items that once occupied that space. I would be a fool not to clear out the vault of my soul in purposeful opposition to all the horrendous fears that scream at the insanity of such an action. And then I must fling open the door of my soul, point to the emptiness I have created, and plead with God to take up residence. And take up residence He gladly does – every time.

And so I intentionally move past life's vendors who offer me nothing eternal, only things that would only fill space I must leave for God. My eyes focused, my heart is set in the grip of determination. I enter the presence of God and walk into the courtyard. The horn blows, and pigeons explode in frenzied flight. I approach the box and whatever thin part of myself I possess, I drop it in. I hand it over. I give it to Him, all of it. And then a weathered life pauses in prayer, thanking Him that I have this opportunity. And I walk away. It is here, in the success of my determination, that God moves, reaches, and then descends. He sees me from the gate and acknowledges my actions as extravagant. Now I am His – totally, as Eddie is His, as this woman was His. And that is the only way to be with God.

Eddie knew that; Eddie was that. As I walked out of his room, I realized the gift I had been given. Holding his file, I looked at the account balance again: 30 cents. I looked at the two thin coins, a gift of totality where nothing was held back in order to sacrifice with safety. No calculating, just abandonment swept the vault of his handicapped life entirely clean so that none of the imperishable riches of heaven would find themselves crowded out by the decaying treasures of this life. And I realized my account ledger needed to read just like that. Just like Eddie's, at the end of the day, the ledger that renders the tally of this life's accumulations needs to read zero.

And when it does, no ledger is large enough to record the riches God pours into that emptied vault.

Pondering Point

"Do not store up for yourselves treasures on earth, where moth and rust destroy, and where thieves break in and steal. But store up for yourselves treasures in heaven ..." (Matthew 6:19-20 NIV). Where are your assets? Our investments speak to our priorities and to the nature of our hearts. They speak to the gods we truly serve despite who we say we worship. And so, where are your assets? How does your ledger read? There is immeasurable power in a sacrificed life. The joy and security we seek is not found in assimilating, but in abandoning; not in gathering but disbursing; holding the treasures of this world loosely so they can be poured out consistently. Thereby, heaven can be poured in. And it is here we find real riches, real living.

A Thought
- Where are my assets?
- What are my assets?
- Do I collect and acquire or do I give excessively?
- Am I willing to abandon my attempts to accumulate life in order that I might gain life?

Chapter 10
A Red Ryder BB Gun

The bowels of Uncle Bill's basement was a winding catacomb of endless adventure for a five-year-old boy. It consisted of dark causeways of aging brick and crumbling mortar that were laced heavily with silky cobwebs that drew together en masse in corners and hung from rough hewn ceiling timbers. It was adventure. Scant windows, foggy with an ancient film of dirt and inattention, sat high, embedded in cold brick walls. Pieces of leftover life were strewn about in various rooms: the discarded and the decaying, things that had fallen into the abyss of time and were waiting to be washed out into the endlessness of eternity past. It was filled with everything the imagination of a young boy could squeeze into its dampness and darkness.

Uncle Bill had an impulsive way about him, those moments when his child side leapt out to do something adventurous, devious – scandalous even, something terribly fun. Standing in the kitchen, Uncle Bill smiled that mischievous smile and motioned me to the basement steps. "I want to show you something," he whispered. He was preparing, it seemed, to do something so fun we were likely to get in trouble for it. How could a five-year-old kid resist? We descended the creaking steps into the bowels of the brick and mortar beast. Flipping a switch caused a bare bulb hanging in a ceramic socket to warm to life, casting an anemic glow that threw pale shadows into the deep dark. Just outside the first room at the bottom of the steps, Uncle Bill stopped. With that elfish smile, he reached behind a door and said, "I want you to see this."

It was dusty and somewhat rusted, but it was absolutely beautiful, the envy of any little boy. If a five-year-old male is ever lustful, it's for one of these. Somehow it was a culmination of all my cowboy fantasies. With it, young boys become heroes, forge fearlessly into uncharted wilderness; singlehandedly repel the enemy; rescue the girl and save the day. Indeed, it was the holy grail of most five-year-old males.

He held it in his thick, calloused hands. Pondering it, he turned it this way and that as if he was savoring a rare treasure. It was clear it had unlocked a floodgate of memories that inundated his mind and swept him in warm currents back in time. There was a reflective pause and then that elfish grin of his as he set up the moment. "Yup, I've had this a long time," he said. "A long time. I shot a few cats with it. I remember shooting a squirrel or two that got into the attic. There were a couple of times I lined up some tin cans and shot them, too ... Yeah, I've had this a long time." My palms were sweating. My forehead was damp with perspiration. My heart was racing. I was standing still but panting anyway. For all I know, I may have been drooling.

And then something transpired I only recognized decades later. It was an ascent to manhood. A rite of passage transpired deep in the darkness and musty air of that cold brick and mortar basement. Hidden away from the rest of the world, it was just me and Uncle Bill. A moment of silence fell, and his eyes met mine. A firm determination had set into them. The child had departed, and the man had returned. The elfish grin had moved aside, being replaced by a hint of squared determination. A passage was indeed developing.

And then, he handed me the BB gun, the Red Ryder BB gun. He set it squarely into my small, untried five-year-old hands. Patting it several times, he said, "Treat it with respect." Then he turned and headed for the steps. I just stood there, aghast and paralyzed. Uncle Bill stopped on the steps, turned and smiled that knowing smile. "Come on." He motioned with a sweep of a large hand. And we ascended the steps together. Not a boy and a man, but a young man and an older man. That day, at that moment, he had begun the process of ushering me into manhood. But he had done more — much more. He had handed me a precious piece of himself. He had left something of himself with me. And I did not know it. I did not understand it until ...

At five, I did not know what cancer was, much less death. And so they sat there, my mom and dad. With the deftness and tenderness that had so marked them, they told me and my brother that Uncle Bill had this thing called cancer. The word "death" was not used, but it was clear. I had had no introduction to death. Its face was strange and imperceptible. Its role and purpose in the landscape of a five-year-old life was too premature to determine. Arriving long before its time, it was alien in a young life where it was yet on a distant horizon far on the other end of life, indiscernible and unintelligible from my vantage point. But whatever it was, it was coming. And it was coming for Uncle Bill.

At five, I watched the face of death as it advanced and laid claim to him. Over the months, it drew him down to an emaciated shadow of himself. The pallet of his life was painted deeply: Pacific war veteran, stalwart, an avid outdoors man, a man of integrity and strength. He became weak and bedridden, his commanding voice diminished to a mere thin whisper that was hardly audible. But he faced death as a man. Not with some fake, superficial macho game-face. But with courage, firm confidence and resolute focus.

One night the word came. A late phone call taken by my father was filled with subdued tones and choked words. I listened as he stammered to find the right words, something my father never struggled with. With shallow steps, he walked into the living room and fell into my mother's embrace. Crouched at the top of the steps as a silent observer, I knew death had arrived, that it had taken Uncle Bill, and that it had fled on black feet. It had left our living room clouded in darkness. It was finally over. I touched my heart and found a hole – my first one. I crawled up the steps, buried myself deep in the thick blankets, and cried myself into a restless sleep.

Deep into the nights, I cried, holding tenaciously to a large stuffed dog until I wore him threadbare. His fur was stained with the tears of a little boy in a deep dark that he knew nothing about, the Red Ryder BB gun at his bedside. Uncle Bill passed into the next life, and I passed out of innocence.

It took several decades before I understood the legacy of Uncle Bill. Standing in that damp basement, he helped me take a step toward manhood. It was a private rite of passage. It was carried out alone, just the two of us. But there was more. He knew he was going to die. Whether he knew specifically or it was simply one of those things of the deep soul, I believe he knew. And when he handed me the Red Ryder BB gun, he was handing me a part of himself. He was indeed leaving something that would outlast him; something that would fill a bit of that hole he would leave; a piece of himself that would roll through the decades ahead in his absence. But even more, he was investing something of himself in that young life. It was something that would grow with me, move with me and serve to shape me. His blessing and a bit of his legacy would do all that and more.

The Passing of a Legacy
The night was thick and heavy. There was a stifling pensiveness that satiated the upper room. It was mysterious indeed. It was the foreboding of something that cannot be identified – only felt. There was a strange juxtaposition of the anticipation of kingship melded with a deep sense of pending disaster. The two feelings wafted around the room as irreconcilable and were, therefore, assumed to be the product of frightened minds and nothing more. One would prevail.

The city had swelled with countless pilgrims. Endless lumbering caravans stretched in thin lines over distant horizons. Perspiring pack animals laden with bulky provisions struggled against heavy loads. Unwieldy and cumbersome, they wound down tight streets. The push and shove of sweaty congestion strained toward a million different destinations at the same time. The braying of donkeys and lowing of cattle mixed and were laced with innumerable conversations in Hebrew, Greek and Aramaic. Squealing children punctuated the air. Vendors were huddled on corners, hawking their wares with sweeping gestures and intrusive voices extolling the fabricated qualities of their product. Streets and alleys coursed with the faithful; the sounds of their lives were mixed into an unintelligible din that rose above and beyond the controlled mayhem.

Then it came, suffocating and suppressing all lesser sounds, reasserting its supremacy. The blast of the ram's horn bellowed from the lofty temple tower. Falling from the precipice, it reminded the coursing minions of the purpose for their journey. Rising thick and weighty, it rolled out of the temple, breeched the temple walls, coursed across the sea of rooftops, and inundated the city streets in a swell of sound. The final bellow surged over the city walls and coursed into the countryside, gradually dissipating among the far-flung hills, valleys and groves that surrounded Jerusalem. Suddenly it fell silent, and the din of compacted humanity resumed.

Evening had fallen without notice. The day began to drift aimlessly into yesterday. Thousands of tents dotted the green hills and valleys surrounding the city. Their rippling cloth structures were scattered as wildflowers in a soft and supple meadow, absorbing the last faint oranges and pastel mauves of a sun having drawn down the backside of a sleepy horizon. Fires sparked to life. The murmuring of a vast contingent of humanity settled and floated intermittently on a tepid breeze that massaged the surrounding hills. Tens of thousands of pilgrims brushed off the excitement and surrendered to the fatigue of celebration. An occasional rooster called into the fading pastels of a day gone sleepy. The bark of dogs wafted lazily across the expanses. The cry of an infant pierced the dusk and elicited the soothing words of a loving mother. Conversations, blurred and faint, were carried on the winds of twilight. Birds settled in variant groves and fluffed feathers to sleep. A flock of pigeons sought a nights roost against the fading mauves of a sleepy dusk.

Three blasts of the trumpet rose in soft succession, declaring the coming of the new day for Israel. Three stars had been seen in the east as tradition declared it. Slowly the trumpet dissipated into the fading light of day, and all fell silent except for the soft murmuring of a world celebrating the Passover feast. A lamb, bitter herbs and unleavened bread were everywhere. All of it harkened to a hurried night in Egypt filled with the wailing of firstborn dead and blood on doorposts. The world soon drifted off to sleep, now resting in anticipation of the weeklong celebration that lay before it.

They had gathered in an upper room painted in the temporal yellows and golds of flickering lamps. The table had been set. The cluster of variant conversations meandered across topics both meaningful and those of simply fill and chatty verbiage. However, all appeared in order except a servant at the door, an obvious omission. There was no one to wash their feet upon their entrance. This oddity created a moment of discomfort and disorientation. Such was the custom of washing one's feet upon entrance into a home that its absence was disturbing and unsettling. Confused glances mark bearded faces. There was no ready explanation, so it was gradually assumed to be an error of omission. But the unease passed, its absence being absorbed into the evening with little trace. The meal proceeded.

"... so he got up from the meal, took off his outer clothing, and wrapped a towel around his waist" (John 13:4 NIV). A departure transpired at this point. Throughout the landscape that spilt from the room, across the city and out beyond into the innumerable tents and temporary abodes scattered as a sea of wildflowers, Passover lambs were being eaten, celebrating the release from bondage. This very celebration was about to fall into irrelevance as the final Passover Lamb prepared for His own sacrifice. Knowing that death was pending; that it was less than 24 hours removed; that it would occur at the blast of the last ram's horns designating the third daily sacrifice on the morrow; the last of the day; the last for eternity ... Jesus knew. And He was about to leave a legacy.

"... he poured water into a basin and began to wash his disciples' feet, drying them with the towel that was wrapped around him" (John 13:5 NIV). There was no immediate response from any of them. It was too far removed from the norm, too illogical. A master never washed the feet of his servants. It was so grossly out of character with their world that they were emotionally hamstrung. But He knelt before each, taking their feet in His hands, caressing them, washing them and then drying them: the Creator washing the feet of the created. The Infinite loving the finite so infinitely that He displaced Himself in order to take that love to a wholly incomprehensible and radically new level. The finite beings seated around that table, when faced with an infinite love, were simply too limited to understand it. It was God shattering the very traditions that men had created to explain Him and contain Him. For in a handful of hours, God would restore the implications of the fall. And He would shatter every box doing it.

And so He moved from disciple to disciple in the silence of the upper room. Flaming torches and the crackling fire were the sole competitors for the silence that saturated the room. The gentle swish of the towel in the basin and the soft sound of dripping water gave the moment a reality. His eyes were soft, but tense. There was within them the culmination of some grand event, the jubilant look of the victor, weighed down and drawn with the anticipated price of the pending victory. An odd mix of irrepressible joy and infinite pain reached out from eyes set deep in love. He was alone in it. He must have been for human comprehension falls desperately short of it. And so He passed on a legacy, a piece of what He would endure and why He would endure it. It was a legacy bearable and understandable enough that mankind can grasp but a thin thread of an infinite act that was only hours away. It was an act that provided a container within which they could place the memory of it, the life of the One who shared it with them, and carry it with them into each of their futures. Finally, He stood erect, and moved to the next. The swish of the towel that day, the thud of the spikes the next: the stuff of sacrifice.

The Legacy of a Legacy

It is not unimaginable to think that, from that moment forward, every time their feet were washed, they saw Jesus stooped over, towel and basin in hand. When the roads were tough at the end of the day, they would see Him. When the path stretched long and dusty, He would be there at road's end in the washing of the feet. And when the world set to rid itself of these apostles and refused to wash their feet, they remembered that neither were His washed that night. I cannot but imagine that this legacy, this memory, gave them hope at the end of many hopeless roads right down to the end of each of their lives.

The Power of Legacy

It was now 40 years later. Thanksgiving had just passed into another year, and the world was decorating itself for Christmas. The roads of my life all seemed to wind from hopelessness to hopelessness. There was nothing on the horizon of my life to draw from, and so I reached back to Uncle Bill. His tombstone had been invaded by encroaching grasses and insensitive weeds. Sitting on a slight rise, little more than a stones throw from a mirrored pond with gliding geese leaving gentle wakes on its glasslike surface, I knelt, brushed back the grass, and pulled away the tenacious weeds. Gently, I placed my hand on the stone and read the inscription 10 or 15 times, wandering back to a brick and mortar basement. I seized a legacy I needed to help me believe in the present and have some shred of hope for the future. I realized that a legacy is not bound to the time in which it was given, but that it is for all time. It is not diminished either by use or by the obstacles that face me. It is a gift that is fresh every time. And I thanked him for the Red Ryder BB gun; for a bit of him in me; for him taking that bit of time to pass something precious along to me; for a legacy.

Pondering Point

Legacy is the gift of a life shared. Whether it's packaged in precious moments or bundled across the expanse of years, a life shared leaves a legacy that gives us points from which to draw strength as we emulate the example of others. It lends us an identity in which to stand when life would cause us to question who we are. It affords us wisdom to borrow unto ourselves from the wisdom displayed by those before us, the courageous examples of others from which we can draw in life's onslaughts. Because others survived and thrived, it is a benchmark that makes hope feasible when all seems hopeless. Theirs is a history that tells us that life is more than simply the difficult realities of the moment, but that life is about a journey traveled by others who have faith that we can finish what they began. The message of the cross is this: I believe in you, and I have an incredible future for you. It is all a remarkable and precious legacy from the past, with an incredible promise for the future.

A Thought
- How can I build my legacy?
- What legacy do I want to create?
- When can I know that the legacy I have to pass on is worthy to build, rather than diminish, something in the life of another?

Chapter 11
On the Roadside

A cleft pallet rendered his words heavy with edges missing from vowels and consonants, softening and muddling many words into verbal oblivion. He was thin and slightly stooped. Coarse hair grew in dense thickets on anemic arms and tender hands. Flat feet slapped the pavement in an awkward rhythm set to the metronome of a broken gait. His feet were set tight in a panicked shuffle when he came to corners, teetering as he rounded them. A thin smear of saliva coated his chin and chapped broad lips. Arms and hands with constant tremors reached out to the world. His was a life both pensive and uncertain, the stuff of darkness.

The most enthralling thing about him was his eyes. There were crystal blue, vivid and deep, sparkling as brilliant gemstones set blazing against thick lashes. Icy, they were yet incredibly warm. Sharp and vibrant, the hues were striking. His were the most beautiful eyes I have ever seen. Yet, for all their stunning beauty, Doug was blind. He groped through his world, an endless black abyss, with tremulous hands outstretched. Tenuous and pensive, his eyes wandered in nothingness, searching, it seemed, to see something in the nothingness. He seemed waiting for his eyes to do what they were supposed to do but couldn't. Somehow, he denied his blindness in the irrational hope that a fleck of color or a streak of light might find some place where blindness forgot to set itself and in the breech, break through. It never happened.

And that is how I met him, that first time. Lost in his crystalline eyes, he placed his hands on my face to discern my features, to paint a picture with his fingertips. By doing so, he filled in the blackness and set against its loneliness something other than the blackness. It was in that first meeting that his fingers saw something in my face. His fingers ascertained much more than the eyes of the sighted. From that moment forward, Doug would be drawn to me. He would become a soul mate, a connection.

Doug was also mentally retarded, the victim of a life that decided to strike twice. Not satisfied with the single theft of his sight, it stole great expanses of his mind as well. The multiple thieveries left his a life pillaged. Others would gather as vultures around a carcass to steal whatever might be left. The road of life up to the moment I met him was marked by physical abuse, sexual assault and gross neglect. He was the product of weak people who found a point of advantage over another and seized it for their own gratification, gorging themselves on the defenseless and satiating their sordid desires on innocence. Such was Doug's life.

The months passed, and I grew to know Doug more. He longed for companionship, but more, he longed to see. Standing in the courtyard of the facility drenched in the rich golden loam of morning sunshine he could not see, he would call my name. He called out from the roadside of a life of shadow and rejection, over and over raising my name until I arrived. Tremulous hands groped toward my voice as I called to him out of his enveloping darkness. Resting his hands on my chest, they would set a palsied-like course to my face and then trace the contours of my features — day after day. Taking my hand and staggering into the darkness of his day, he would pull me to some object or place, asking me to describe a multitude of things from flowers, to bricks, to candy wrappers, to umbrellas, remembering and recalling each description with uncanny and precise accuracy. Doug was building into the folds of his mind what his eyes would not deliver. He was painting a famished canvas desperate for an image borrowed from the eyes of another. His was a life relegated to the roadside of life, but he refused to stay there.

Another on the Roadside
Sounds provided no hues. They threw no shadows, and they splashed no color. Dimension was absent. Shape, form and texture could not be seized from language or apprehended from sound. It could all be explained, but it could not be experienced. Words floated in as markers, giving some vague shape to something shapeless. Pieces of the world passed by and were snatched. Sounds drifted in. His eyes were dead. He had no means by

which to reach out and seize the world of light, color, shapes and shadows. He was a pauper, left only to grasp the pieces of the world thrown his way on the roadside of life.

Sounds and words are not eyes, so he sat on the roadside, apprehending the passing world by dissecting sound and grasping at tidbits of the melody and the dissonance that played round about him. Piecing together a world he had no basis from which to comprehend. Tattered he sat. Frayed wraps, sparse with gangling threads, flirted with an occasional breeze. His hair was a tangled mass; oily and coarse, it framed a weather-worn face. Skin thick, time had plowed deep furrows embedded with a gritty mixture of dirt and sticky sweat. His eyes were hollow, open to nothing but darkness. They traced the sounds that moved about him, shifting and following them as they drifted. His head was up slightly, canted just a bit, digesting every morsel of sound that the world threw his way.

A cup was held out. Hope was held out. He called into the darkness and pleaded his cause, his fear, his hopelessness and his pain, hoping that the darkness would respond to some piece or part of that which he threw out into it. He hoped it would yield something that would get him through the darkness of the day. His cup followed the sounds that passed by, shadowing the footfalls coming toward him in the form of crunching gravel and muted conversation. He hoped that, somewhere in them, there was a crumb for his body and his soul. A passerby paused, extracted a weathered pouch, rummaged its sparse contents and dropped a thin coin into the waiting cup. His fingers leapt, quickly scouring the inside of the cup and locating the coin. He fingered it to determine its worth and then tucked it deep in a secure fold in his robe. Immediately, the cup was extended again and the pleading resumed.

This was his life. A meager existence was begged on a roadside from a world he could not see. It was a world so much more than he could comprehend or imagine — so very much more. But he was blind. The cup was extended again and again. The cries of a beggar filled the air, hoping for but a morsel.

I Inhabit the Roadside
I live on the roadside. And I too am blind: sometimes more, sometimes less. It is not visual blindness as much as it is spiritual. Bereft of spiritual

eyes, I think I see when I do not. I hate the blindness, its evidence becoming strikingly clear in my turmoil, pain and trials. I think I see, but God draws me into times of devastation, and I realize that, in the horror and hell, I do not. I am utterly and abjectly blind. I'm blind even to the fact that I am without sight, which is the essence of true blindness. There is so much more going by me on the road of life, but I sit at its edge, on the gravel fringes, with my cup in hand, straining to hear, to know, to see what is going by on that road. I sit there begging for some morsel to satisfy a bit of the hunger of life, realizing that only God can call me onto that road and there give me sight. And so, I am on the roadside, blind, cup in hand, calling out. We all are the blind beggar.

It was humid and lush. The road winded downward, meandering below sea level into tropical Jericho. It was an ancient city with a history 5,000 years old even before Jesus set foot in it. His journey however, was eternal, rendering its history a slight vapor quickly dissipated. The gates of Jericho lay ahead. Jerusalem on the horizon and Golgotha was just beyond that. The crescendo of His earthly journey was rising. Forces, both physical and spiritual, were marshaling and assembling. All was preparing for a horrendous clash that was drawing ever near. He had just recounted events to come with His disciples. The meaning of the coming events remained hidden from them, for they were too powerful, too consuming, and too awful to be digested by this handful of mismatched men cavorting through history with the Messiah. But for now, they drew near to Jericho.

The sounds were different. They were not reminiscent of the typical traffic that flowed in and out of the city to which his ears were so accustomed. The blind beggar lowered his cup; leaned forward; closed blind eyes; and strained to focus with intent. He reached out to grasp every slight sound that wafted down the road and brushed across his leathered face. It was unlike anything else. A crowd ... yes, but there had been crowds before. There was electricity in the sounds, something completely unusual was pressing up the road, winding, and then cresting a slight roll in the landscape. It began descending toward him. It was the sound of humanity alive, not about any sort of business or off in a hurried rush. It was not headed somewhere with a somewhere focus, but it was alive and vibrant in the moment. Each step was marked with enthusiasm. Eyes were not needed to see God afoot.

He reached out, groped and yelled into the blackness, "Who is coming? Who is this about to pass by?" The tenor of his voice was alive with the excitement of anticipation, of wanting to join a world he could not see. He shouted again.

Annoyed, someone retorts, "Jesus of Nazareth is passing by" (Luke 18:37 NIV). Instantly, it was clear. It was impossible. Stories of Him had meandered down this road before, wild tales, but at the same, titillating and plausible. But this, this was no story. This was He whom the stories were about.

The sound of footsteps magnified in intensity. A multitude of voices in a linguistic stew melded with increasing volume. Words once muffled became clearer. Word spread, surged, and rolled up the road ahead of Him. "It is Jesus."

In a moment, the entourage was upon him. His mind raced and the words blurted and leapt from his mouth: "Jesus, Son of David, have mercy on me!" (Luke 18:38 NIV) His plea was thrust into the darkness and thrown out onto the road. Sound was all he knew. It was the only medium of communication, and so he shouted. His words penetrated the edges of the crowd and rippled inward. Those on the periphery caught his words and rebuked him. They attempted to thwart his efforts to reach into their world. But the world of sounds was his domain. So he shouted again, his pleas penetrating the crowd and falling, finally, on the ears of Jesus. And then the world stopped.

There was no hesitation, for faith always catches the ear of God. "Bring him here." An order, it was immediate and firm. Several stirred and headed for the man. He was raised to trembling feet. Unsteady and stumbling, he caught his balance. His cup dropped and lay spilt on the roadside. Its role in his life was concluded, for begging would end here. Roadsides and cups: in a moment, they would all be things of the past. He stepped away from it all, his arms outstretched, held on both sides by strangers. Attempting to apprehend the sounds around him as he pierced the edges and cut into the bowels of the crowd, he was lost in the noise. Then there was a voice that was beyond it all, that carried a tone and resonated of power he had never heard before – a single voice. All other sound vanished in the wake of that voice. It was oddly soft for its power, confident but commanding. The starkness of the authority was exhilarating and yet terribly frightening, richly warm but defiantly powerful all at once. He had never heard anything like it. It was humanity punctuated and laced with the divine.

"What do you want me to do for you?" (Luke 18: 41 NIV) was the question. The words leapt out, both in their abruptness and their unquestioning ability to do whatever was asked of them. They were strong enough to bear even a request of the impossible. The crowd was silent. There were now no sounds other than the shuffling of feet, the flapping of robes caught in the slight breeze, and the sound of a miracle waiting on tiptoe.

His mind raced through the back alleys of darkness, groping and poverty, a cup and a few scattered coins. In those places, there were only a few scant morsels of food, of life and of hope; roadsides but never being on the road. Never apprehending the road or what traveled it, he was doomed as a blind bystander. Counting on the generosity of the road and those who walked it, he was helpless. It all coalesced and then the answer leapt to his lips. "Lord, I want to see" (Luke 18:41 NIV).

The Cry of My Heart

That is my cry. "Lord, I want to see!" I don't want to think that I see. I don't want to substitute my blind perception of sight for His. I want to abandon my assumptions of sight and seeing altogether and really see. I want to possess eyes that see as God sees. I want to ask for something I can't even remotely comprehend, something I can't ask for of my own because it exceeds the depth and breadth of my experience and my knowledge. I want to drop my many cups, leave them strewn on the roadside, get up, stumble into the crowd, fall at His feet, and plead the impossible. "Lord, I want to see!"

There was a pause. He was seeing before he even saw. There was a smile on the face of this Jesus. The blind man could hear it. There was a joy exuding in restoring sight to the blind and life to the lifeless. Jesus drew a confident breath, giving Himself a moment to revel in a life about to be restored. Lightly, He touched the man's shoulder and stared into eyes that could not stare back, those eyes void of light. He prepared for a double miracle: eyes that were about to see and a soul that would actually see first. With a voice saturated with love, He said, "Receive your sight; your faith has healed you" (Luke 18:42 NIV).

The blind man shuddered and stumbled backward. He held tentative hands over his eyes and cried out. Blinding light assaulted him. An explosion of deep color detonated across an empty canvas. Rich hues, textures, shadow and shapes deluged his world. A tidal wave coursing through eyes restored threw him to his knees. There were no words. He was paralyzed in his attempts to associate his world of sound with that of sight. It was impossible. There was too much, and it was all too fast.

And so he resorted to the only thing that made sense; that gave him grounding; that provided a benchmark in a world turned upside down. He resorted to sounds, to words, to that which identified his world only moments earlier. He praised God, ceaselessly and endlessly, erupting on shaking knees in abject poverty. It was not in material poverty, but the authentic poverty, the real poverty of a fallen human being realizing the terrible inadequacy of their humanness in the face of an infinite, loving God. A gasp arose from the crowd. It is an impossible attempt to digest the impossible. And it is realized — God is amongst us. There was no rebuke from the crowd this time. Rather, they joined the man once blind. They partnered with him on the road. Praise was raised and caught on the wind. It drifted across the road, throughout the countryside and across history.

My Encounter with Sight
When vision comes, I too am on my knees. There is no other place to be. There is nothing else that is appropriate. Seeing as God sees renders all else blindness. I am faced with the striking reality that I had presumed my blindness to be sight, thinking myself as possessing that which I did not possess. Real blindness is the absence of the knowledge that one is blind. And most of us are, in this sense, blind in totality.

And then I see the road. I never see it all, but I see it. And I can see the roadside as well with my cups strewn there. It is but a pitifully narrow slice of life that I inhabited in my blindness and ignorance. And I will travel with Jesus now – always in a state of praise. I am ever close to the hem of His garment; in step with Him; tracing His every move, His every turn. I am ever delighted by His smile and always captivated by His glance. I am forever lost in His presence.

The mass moved and resumed the momentum of the journey out towards the gates of Jericho: one step closer to Jerusalem and one stride nearer

Golgotha. One minute closer to an empty tomb that would repeat this moment, this instance, in the lives of untold billions. And what a remarkable moment it was!

God's Eyes
One day Doug sat on a park bench outside his room. In trembling hands, he held a single flower, a bird of paradise. As I sat next to him, he said, "I know what this looks like." This blind, mentally retarded young man refused to sit along the roadside of life. Doug had gathered all of our assorted moments together. I had painted explanations of the wonders of life across the darkened canvas of his mind, drawing from the palate of words the colors and hues of the mind and painting them the best I knew how. And so he described the flower in rich detail. Then, taking me by the hand, he pulled me across the courtyard, explaining object after object after object in the richest of detail. I was stunned. I could not fathom him as blind; such was the complexity, the passionate romance, and the sheer exhilaration that embodied each detailed description. He saw better than I did, for the heart always discerns more sharply than the eyes. Doug refused not to see even when his eyes refused.

Doug refused to live life on the roadside. His handicaps were enough to keep him there, but his indomitable spirit precluded them all. When my time with Doug came to an end, he was living more than most people I know. On my final day with Doug, he said, "You know, I can see now!"

And I said, "Maybe some day you can teach me to see."

Pondering Point
Most of us prefer blindness, for it gives us permission to sit along the roadside of life. Even more than permission, our own blindness keeps us from realizing we are there in the first place. In time, blindness is presumed to be vision. And at that point, our blindness has become our understanding and definition of sight. And with this presumed sight, we no longer realize our blindness. Do we really want to see? Indeed, it can be transforming.

A Thought
- Do I see? Or is what I see my perception of what real sight is?
- Am I daring enough to really see, knowing that what I see may demand more of me?

- Am I courageous enough to see the real world that lies beyond me and then to set my feet to that road?

Chapter 12
A Blizzard of Blossoms

As a child, I reveled in them while they lived, their life spilling into me as I rested in their boughs. As a young adult, I cried over them at their deaths. And as a person, I am forever changed in that they miraculously live again.

Spring is the beginning beyond the end. It is the unexpected addendum to death that is, in reality, the first chapter of a never-ending story that leaves the rest of the preceding tale as a brief footnote. Spring says real life can only be lived on the heels of death and whatever transpired before is only the vaguest precursor. It is an eternal reality manifest in a natural cycle, baring eternity exposed in advance of our own arrival there.

As a child, I spent countless spring mornings lying in the tender emerald grass, engulfed in a sea of dandelions that seemed as spots of brilliant yellow pigment liberally splattered from an artist's palette. As the morning's sun peeked over a yawning horizon, I would stare up through branches dense with fresh, white cherry blossoms, spring's herald of fall's coming bounty. Life was emerging not just for life's sake or for some show of resilience, but life to perpetuate and build upon itself in the eternal expansion of life that will someday eclipse death altogether.

The sun seemed more golden in the morning, its lucid brilliance not yet having been diminished by the demands of the coming day. Its opulent rays, having reached over the horizon, fell on the cherry tree as a pure golden rain, dripping from the snow white cherry blossoms in 24-carat translucent droplets. Its light backlit each petal, transforming the cherry trees' branches into a dazzling white blizzard of blossoms.

The clean, buoyant breezes of spring ran not far behind the advancing sun. They drew their warm fingers gently through the perfumed clouds of petals, teasing out robust aromatic waves and sending them softly breaking across my face. I found my body embraced in an invisible sweetness that spilled out beyond where I lay and gently rolled across the broad green stretches of tender grass.

Caught in this rich, airy bouquet, dozens of mesmerized bees droned trance-like from blossom to blossom. Legs heavy with nectar's golden dust, they sampled spring's sweet bounty until their transparent wings could barely lift them, finally lumbering off to unload their treasure at some secret destination. Their activity created a soothing hum of satisfaction as if nature was taking a moment to take pleasure in itself. I would lie there, close my eyes, and breathe in every drop of the flood of life that washed in sweet charismatic swells over my soul.

By the time my adult years rolled around, the magnificent cherry trees had aged and diseased beyond redemption. Their once muscular trunks had fallen prey to the rot of age and the scourge of ants. Limbs that once invited young boys to endless adventure in a leafy canopy and a blue sky beyond creaked with years that had compromised their strength and altogether silenced the adventuresome tenor of their voices. Springs were now met with a few anemic leaves scattered across vast canopies now rendered largely bald. They were skeletal, having no energy and too little life to respond to the soft summons of spring. Only a muted handful of blossoms dotted the multitudinous, starkly barren branches. Sap seeped from deep fissures that etched jagged lines up thick trunks. The trees wept, it seemed, in sticky rivulets of sorrow out of the futility of naked canopies. Death loomed. They seemed to know it.

The waiting for death is dictated by the assumptions about death: the silent vigil of finality, death being irrevocably tied to loss. In reality, it is not the loss of the object. It is all about our loss in light of that ending. The end looms bigger than the beginning that it spawns. Therefore, an end is all we can see. Sorrow does not afford us vision beyond the horizon where loss sets. Neither does faith. Faith, however, causes us to rely on Someone who sees beyond the darkening edges of the horizon. And He says that what is a sunset on this side of it all is a sunrise on the other.

One fateful fall afternoon, with chainsaws in hand and lumps in our throats, we approached the old trees. Their horizon was darkening. With a single pull of the cord, one of the chainsaws roared to life, immediately joined by a second in a two-cycle chorus of death. Both united to spew a caustic blue-white cloud of exhaust into branches that, for so many seasons, had emanated rich perfumed clouds quite different than those. With a deafening roar, the chainsaws' ravaging teeth set about the business of finalizing the loss. In tandem, they bit into the ancient trunks, ruthlessly spewing bits of the tree's heartwood in all directions. Flakes and shavings blanketed the sullen ground around us as spots of brown pigment liberally splattered from death's pallet.

With their aged trunks fatally undercut, one by one their wooden columns teetered, slow and almost reverently, as if resisting death would also be resisting the life that would follow. There was, it seemed, a willing obedience to a larger plan. With a deft measure of grace, they fell helplessly to the very ground that had been a privileged recipient of their blossoms for so many springs. With a few brief swipes of the chainsaws, the trees were rendered a lifeless stack of cordwood.

The trees' histories, written in their many rings, lay naked and exposed at the end of each piece, citing the closing of one drama to make way for the next. Shutting off the chainsaw, I paused for a moment and wondered if the rings that marked each year of growth remembered the little boy who, for so many years, sat enthralled under their branches, or were they now little more than dead wood? Did they know? I set down the chainsaw, turned toward a darkening horizon and cried.

A Bit of Eternity

The sun threw a few last scant rays over the western horizon. Dusk assumed its place, obediently keeping pace with a sleepy sun, rolling up in its darkening folds the remnants of an exhausted day. The flurry of the Passover was settling over the city, drifting and then dissipating in the deepening dusk engulfing Jerusalem. The murmur of celebratory humanity caught in its own exhaustion was sleepy and heavy. The day had been filled with celebration and sacrifice; ritual and rite; the myriad mingling of multiple cultures descending on this city to remember, reflect and recall.

It was a celebration of unleavened bread, bitter herbs, blood on doorposts, and a hasty expulsion by a nation that had awakened to firstborn death. But for now, in the extending and deepening shadows engulfing the landscape, the city settled.

Another stream ran through the current of that particular Passover. It had, at that moment, pooled in Gethsemane, east across the city from there. Great drops of blood dripped from a forehead, God in angst. Jesus was aware of the plan long before it unfolded, replacing the anxiety of speculation with the chilling horror of certainty. He knew soldiers would seize Him and channel the current though the city.

It would flow through the house of the high priest, elegant and ornate. Then it would shift north, through the Sanhedrin, deluged in the garments of tradition and religious rigor. From there, it would flow through Herod's palace, to the west. The marbled walls were rubbed soft in the milky thin moonlight. Pilate would step into its waters in the Antonia towers. Then, coursing the Via Dolorosa, it would crest on Golgotha, its pending terror northwest just outside the city wall. It would finally ebb and pool in a chiseled, borrowed tomb, a bit beyond there. Three days later, a spring of life would surge from the rock walls. But, at that moment, He was in Gethsemane. The soldiers were on their way, possessing an edict from the religious leaders to kill God. The collision and resulting turbulent headwaters of a plan launched at the fall of mankind was moments from happening.

What was Golgotha like the night before His death? I wonder. It is not recorded in scripture. Oh, to stand there that night, knowing what would unfold directly across the city, knowing what would unfold on this crest on the morrow.

The moon rose, washing the hill in a breathless pallor of death. The call of a roosting bird briefly broke the silence. Settling, silence absorbed the hill once more. Various implements of death left by careless soldiers lay strewn about. Bones bleached in the moonlight cried with no voice, silently screaming the horror of those last moments. No one heard because no one listened. Its summit was saturated with lives lost. Footprints of the dead cover its alien landscape. Blood, an accounting of lives lost, lay thick and coagulated deep in the gravelly soil. It lay strewn and spattered across rocks as panicked bodies were pushed into the chasm of death. Fingers desperately clawed the precipice, terrified in finding the battle useless, life being forced out of them despite their frenzied efforts to hold on. Cries, moans, pleading and gasping marked the deaths that transpired there. Babbling minds seized in surrender to the caustic black face of death peered full faced into the abyss with shrieks that described what their souls saw. And then … the fall.

Always, silence fell. Eventually death reigned – eventually. The abyss was repeatedly satisfied. Here on Golgotha life would terminate. Whatever the myriad stories that had passed before the arrival on this hill, the final page was written here. Innumerable books were closed and sealed, forever lost to the greater story of the ages. Lives and their accompanying stories dissipated in the backwash of history and were swept away in the undertow of time – gone. Such was the horror of that hill. On that night, it was particularly poignant because, the next day, the incomprehensible would happen. On that hill, the infinite would surrender to death. God – would – die.

The moonlight had thickened a bit, washing across the hill in a pasty wash. On the far side of the city, the soldiers had likely seized Him. The river had set its course from that place to this one. The night to come would be filled with beatings, accusations, lies fabricated in the pit of hell and vomited into that river. Lacerations and contusions would mark that night, mark it deeply. He would drag a cross onto that silent hill, and there He too would die. Like all the others – eventually. And it was only hours away.

From Golgotha, this river would meander in rivulets of sorrow into a tomb just west of there. The final page would be written. The book would seem closed. Sealed like all the rest, left to be caught in the backwash of history and the undertow of time. But it would be different this time. No one suspected it, for God never died before.

A Gateway

Is not the faint voice of the eternal to be heard in death? Death leads to life, even in this temporal existence of ours. Somewhere, somehow, something arises out of the ashes of our losses that reminds us that nothing ever ceases; nothing ever vanishes. God is always creating, even in the midst of devastation. His hand is incessantly recreating, renewing, rewriting and revising faster than the devastation from whose ashes He draws the raw material from which to recreate. Always! "I am making everything new!" (Revelation 21:5 NIV) It's a declarative statement that demands the passing of the old to make way for the creating of the new. The discarded shards, shreds and remnants of that which has died and passed represent the stuff from which the new is miraculously shaped. And there lies the most profound of promises: The passing of the old is not a tragic end in itself. Rather, it is a step to something new. It's a glorious promise that, when set starkly against our immutable losses, gives us immutable hope. Death is an end that only marks a beginning and exists only for that beginning, a promise that sows life with deep meaning and death with profound purpose.

"I tell you the truth, unless a kernel of wheat falls to the ground and dies, it remains only a single seed. But if it dies, it produces many seeds" (John 12:24 NIV). Thereby, it produces life that is in excess of and superior to the death that birthed it. A sunset on one side is a sunrise on the other. What was to transpire on that hill bathed in moonlight would establish this principle. It would declare it and forever seal it. History will pivot on that hill for every tomorrow. And thank God it does.

Winter and Spring ... Again

With winter's snows having begun to seize the land once again, the cherry trees' trunks were left until spring's soft ground would allow us to fully uproot them. That was the plan anyway, errantly conceived out of the assumption that loss is just that: loss and no more. Into winter's dreary months we marched, frequently looking into the backyard where the old trees had been and to where I had spent so many wonderful spring mornings as a child. A gaping hole marked the landscape – just like the landscape of my heart.

Winter came and winter went. One day, the snow having long vanished, I wandered back to the old cherry trees. The tender emerald grass had blanketed the landscape, bidding me come and lie in it once more. The artist had again returned from his prolonged absence. Taking his palette in hand, he engulfed me in a sea of dandelions that seemed as spots of brilliant yellow pigment liberally splattered from his prolific palette. In its unfailing consistency, the sun stretched its golden fingers over a sleepy, spring-laden horizon. I lay there and realized it was once again what it had been for so many, many wonderful years.

However, it suddenly became immensely and wrenchingly empty as I realized there were no branches through which to watch spring unfold. The sun still seemed more golden in the morning, but there were no snow white cherry blossoms from which its opulent rays would drip. Its light searched for the soft, white petals in order to marvelously backlight each one. Instead, the falling torrent of golden light fell helplessly through the air and formed dismayed, luminous puddles on the ground all around me.

As with years past, the clean, buoyant breezes of spring reached out with their warm fingers, but they found no perfumed clouds of petals. My senses desperately reached out as well, but there were no robust aromatic waves to softly break across my face and generously roll across the broad stretches of green. Anticipating spring's nectar, the bees lumbered in from their secret destinations only to circle in confusion and then depart, leaving me in silence. My heart turned within me. The magnificent blizzard of blossoms was truly gone.

I stood and turned to leave. As I did, I glanced at the two stumps that seemed to be nothing more than grave markers. Graying monuments to an irretrievable past. A piece of death reminding me of what had been. Death sometimes haunts us even after it has passed unto itself. But there, stubbornly poking their way up from each stump, was a single, slim stem. It was not possible. I squinted and moved closer. On that tiny stem, there protruded several plump buds. In time, they would produce a few small leaves and a small cluster of beautiful white blossoms. I knelt beside the old stumps and gently fingered the single stems. Wiping back the tears, I realized what had been dead was alive again. The beauty of what had been was to be once more. Death was a gateway to life. A sunset on this side is a sunrise on the other.

Today, some 25 years after that wonderful moment of discovery, the cherry trees have completely regenerated themselves. They stand taller than they had during those many years that I, as a child, had sat underneath their magnificent branches. Now each spring, some three or more decades removed from those dreamy childhood mornings, I wander out to the old trees, lie in the thick grass, engulfed in a sea of dandelions, and once again revel in that most spectacular white blizzard of blossoms.

The tomb surged empty. The waters would gather, foam, and rise as an eternal torrent, bursting out of that tomb three days later. It would crest in a tidal wave that would sweep all the world for all time, finally ebbing into the shoals of eternity, rendering Golgatha forever useless. Death can come – and it will. But it is now beaten. It has been seized, changed, and reshaped as a gateway to the eternal where loss is irrepressibly offset by the immutable life that now springs from it.

Pondering Point
We associate death with permanence. Losses are seen as losses. Our view is canted by the finite world in which we live. Too often, we don't associate and apply the eternal to life and living. The eternal is an extension beyond what our eyes see. What ends here begins there. What was gained, shaped, molded and crafted goes on, as did Jesus, as did the two cherry trees.

A Thought
- Can I begin to think beyond the temporal to the eternal?
- Am I willing to see the finite world in which I live as a river that rolls into eternity and beyond?
- How will that change my view of loss?
- How will that change my view of life?

Chapter 13

Why Are You Doing This?

I drew back in my seat with hands hard pressed on the steering wheel; nine patients in nine hours. My mind was a mushy mix of thoughts, theories, grief and pain. I was exhausted, attempting to bring some shred of hope, some thin glint of light, some reason for living to those who daily filled my office. Facing the deluging torrent of human pain, agony, degradation and futility day in and day out: that is my job. That is what I do. And on days like that one, I wonder if I do it effectively at all. Do I make even the most imperceptible difference? Numbed, I leaned my head back on the headrest and navigated the flood of cars heading home as was I. I was lost in traffic while lost in thought.

On those days, I question my worth and my value. I question if indeed I bring anything worthwhile to the lives around me. I ask penetrating and painful questions about the validity of my life. The scourge of the human condition is to question the value of the human condition. Do I possess anything worthwhile or valuable? Do I count for something that gives legitimacy to my existence? Am I worth the resources I use to sustain myself? Such days prompt such thoughts. They pour through the ruptures forged by my frequently low self-esteem, deluging my mind, flooding my heart. That day they spilled across the seat of my car and pooled in puddles at my feet. The thoughts pounded me like incessant waves at the forefront of an approaching hurricane with all the force of an emotional tidal surge and they screamed, "Am I worth anything?" The traffic thinned, and my mind wandered.

My Worth in His Action

A thud, deep, thick and thunderous, pounded the air. Somehow, it rolled beyond the cavernous street and out into eternity. Sweat and blood spattered across the arid dirt and gravel. Dust rose from the impact, drifting and edging into dissipation. A hand, palm down, struck the ground as an exhausted effort to brace the fall and steady the weight proved futile. The crossbeam cantered, tilted and leaned. The draw of gravity on dense timbers was broad and irreversibly heavy. Blood, caked and coagulated in gouging lacerations, was embedded with the sticky filth of sweat, dirt, and the seeping of fresh blood. Exhaustion was all there was. The body was sapped from a night of horrendous beating. Death was already well on its way. He fell. His hair was grimy with sweat; a fiendish embellishment of thorns was tangled amidst clumps of stringy hair sopped in crimson. He lay facedown in the dirt. His breath — heavy, labored.

The crowd was a sordid mix of empathy and deep angst at the immutable suffering God. Others were jeering, taunting and engaged in raucous mocking: kicking dirt, throwing gravel, and hurling leaden insults that struck Him. Some were drawn by the titillating itch of curiosity, beckoning to them, raising them up on tiptoe with necks outstretched. The callousness of mankind was fully manifest and set against the love of God bleeding in the gravel. The pure, undiluted evil of the adversary seized the scene. It was venomous and toxic. The wound had been inflicted; the spiritual poison was now running through the very veins of God Himself.

Centurions, the veterans of innumerable crucifixions, pushed the beams upright, grabbed an unsuspecting bystander and thrust him into the street. Confounded, he stumbled and stepped to the center of the hard packed roadway and to the center of history itself. Pensively, he set his own hand against the beam and steadied it. He glanced into the mangled face and caught a glimpse, a flash of perfection that was wholly unmatched by the scene. It was a glimmer of something greater than everything that defined that moment and swirled around it in that street. A covert invasion was in process; none in the crowd suspected it. The price of the invasion was indescribable. It was a great assault, far beyond the comprehension of the crowd. Something about this prophet was different.

The moment was suddenly broken as the centurions grabbed the dying man and pulled Him away from the cross – only momentarily. Simon shouldered the beams and leveled the weight. His sandals pressed moist in the slough mix of blood and dirt. He drew a breath and then stepped.

Somehow, I was there. All of us were. It was a pivotal event that extended the impossible to all of us. My soul is so desperate for what it offered, for what it meant, even though I would not feel its effects for thousands of years. But I was there, for the act is timeless. It is rooted in eternity, not in the constant journey of the sun from one horizon to the other or the passing of the seasons that left this event to sit forever only in the confines of that day, of days like today. In His heart, I was there.

Why?
And it would be at that moment, on His way to the cross. Before it was too late. Before the spikes truly sealed the death that was well on its way. Before the clock began to tick off the seconds of those last three hours of His life. Before the thief, the sponge, the sour wine, the mockery, the words "my God." Before all of that, I want to kneel with Him at that moment, on that street, on my knees, prostate beside Him. I want my face level with His, my hands claw-like in the grit and dirt right beside Him. I want to shout, "Why are you doing this? I'm not worth it! Do you hear? I'm not worth it!" The core of my humanity screaming its worthlessness, that You, God, are somehow insane for doing this for me.

"Simply let me cease to exist. Cast me into the abyss of nothingness until any memory of me is extracted from every mind, every heart — even Your heart. Unwrite the history that brought me to this moment. Erase me. Annihilate me. Send me beyond oblivion, outside of creation itself. But don't do this. Please, do not do this. Don't ... because I love you too much." Impassioned and desperate, the created finds himself pleading for the life of the Creator. It is an odd disparity.

Would He smile? I doubt it. That was a moment of eternal horror and infinite seriousness. He was truly alone. It had passed out of human hands. He had unsheathed a sword and raised a banner, thrusting it deep into the ground, unfurled. His feet were firmly planted. The challenge was declared. I will take it back! There was before Him a sweeping spiritual battlefield, epic in scope. Hills were lacquered black and thick with horrendous demonic hoards girding themselves for battle. The advance had begun in a manger 33 years earlier. It would not stop. It was to the death.

Would He somehow acknowledge my words? Maybe. But the task was bigger than my words and infinitely larger than my shallow human demand. Would He press on with the insistence that I am too valuable to cast into nothingness? That it is already decided? It is beyond discussion or debate. His eyes were blackened and deeply swollen. Blood was trickling, seeping from a cruel crown and tracing errant lines around hollow sockets. But His eyes were firm and profoundly resolute. They were human, but much more. Through lips, swelled, cracked and bloodied, He might have murmured the words, "I love you too much." If not, He was thinking them in His soul, shouting them on that spiritual battlefield, shouting them for all of us.

The cross began to move. Centurions lifted a shredded body to its feet. He stumbled off, listing under the effects of scourging, blood loss, and the sins of mankind. His attention was there on that hill, preparing to do final battle with the minions of hell and the sin of man. The crowd moved along, culling a mix of confusion, hatred and simple spectators. Those who loved Him and those who hated Him found equal place in the crowd. There were those who didn't know Him but had found themselves consumed in the frenzy of a mindless crucifixion. Each one was the sole reason for the battle none of them could see. Though he was limping, a javelin prodded Him. He stumbled again, paused, regained His balance and resumed. And so it was, the journey to the hill and to death

My Worth ... My Role
I am not worth what He did, not in what I see in myself. It's absurd. I hate the thought. Yet, I am, at the same time, captivated by it. I sense a worth in myself I cannot even remotely comprehend. I am taken beyond myself and forced to see something in me that my own eyes cannot: the image of God stamped on my soul that makes me something of infinite worth. I am the son of the King who has forgotten his sonship so entirely I am convinced of my impoverishment. My soul is held hostage to an enemy force I cannot reckon with, that insists I am impoverished. My liberation is a must. It is an eternal non-negotiable. The sword is unsheathed. The banner is planted and unfurled in the winds of eternity. The cry is raised and the assault engaged. And the purpose? You and I.

It is not about what I am ... or what I bring ... or what I do ... or what kind of day I have. It's about who God is. I am valuable because "I am fearfully and wonderfully made" (Psalm 139:14 NIV). He alone conceived of me, and then He alone crafted me. I am His handiwork, the product of the Master Artist and a manifestation of His limitless genius. The thoughts lift me and lighten my mind. The traffic has cleared and so have my thoughts. It doesn't all feel so heavy and hopeless now. My value is beyond what I do; rather, it is based on whose I am. And Him to whom we belong assessed our value as equal to His life.

The thud on that raucous street deep in the city was to be followed by another series of thuds on a hilltop of death hours later. Deep, thick, thunderous even. The others were to follow on a hilltop as spikes were driven. Another thud as the cross was raised and dropped. A thud as the rock sealed the tomb. And a final thud as the stone was rolled away. The battle was fought with infinite angst, the blood of the infinite God, and ended in infinite victory. It was fought for you and for me because we are worth the battle.

Pondering Point

We don't want to admit it, but most of us don't like ourselves a whole lot. Once we get past the many fronts and facades we put up to spruce up our image and get down to us, we often don't like what we see. Self-images are destroyed by hands, both intentionally and unintentionally. They're destroyed by those who are supposed to love us – and those who have no such compulsion. Our lives become splintered on the rocks of betrayal, abandonment, abuse, neglect and other assorted maladies inflicted from without and absorbed within. Our self-image is taken captive, mirroring and applying to ourselves the abuse others have perpetrated upon us, assuming that their response to us is a genuine reflection of our worth and value. Most often, it is not. The sole benchmark that bespeaks your value is the action of Jesus on your behalf. No other actions matter. We must see our reflection in His work, not in the other myriad voices that would diminish us.

A Thought
- From what or whom have I derived my sense of value?
- Have I assumed the actions of others toward me as a commentary on my value or can I see those actions as reflective of that person's issues?
- Am I willing to look fully into the cross and apply that action as

fully and comprehensively indicative of my value?

Chapter 14
And It Is Saturday

She smeared deep red lipstick in thick layers over wrinkled lips. Having been applied with trembling hands, the waxy crimson set an errant course, wandering off the edges onto adjacent skin. A dusting of rosy blush gave an aura of life to cheeks washed white and fallen with the weight of time. A lengthy string of fake pearls, faded in disappointment, encircled the tired folds of her aged neck. Thinned by time and colored a light ashen gray by the wash of pain, her hair was fluffed and sprayed into weak curls. Sparse locks set about her head in thin and precarious waves. A powder blue dress fell over a body drawn down from assorted maladies both physical and emotional. Her physique was emaciated beyond fragility. Loose skin was thrown over a bony frame with little flesh to draw it firm. A few last touches in a foggy mirror, and she headed for the door — as she had hundreds of times before. It would be the same.

I didn't especially like working the adult unit. It wasn't that I feared working with psychotic adults. Rather, the shifts were predictably unpredictable, rending eight hours an experience that sporadically hurled and halted itself through moments of jarring chaos sometimes controlled, but more often, uncontrolled. I took blood pressure and played a litany of worn videos that had been seen a hundred times, but never remembered. Catatonic patients sat steeped in drooling stupors in corners — living out their lives in deep shadows from which they could not escape.

Cries of women traumatized by non-existent horrors rolled down sterile linoleum hallways, their shrieks a response to petrifying images of wild minds unleashed and unfettered. So many lives were seized helplessly in the grip of minds awash in an irrepressible torrent of life at its worst multiplied to insanity. I read to patients in order to calm rampant thoughts.

There was always a series of restraints where a handful of staff would tie down a convulsing body that, left to its own devices, would inflict injury – or death. A weathered nurse would apply medication and chart yet another tragedy. We observed the patient as the drug asserted the control the patient could not, slowly loosening the belts and cuffs one by one as the medication did what it was intended to do. Within moments, we were doing it all over again with another patient seized by psychosis and lost in a labyrinth of lunacy. It may be that insanity is the realization that sanity is a hope forever deferred, a longing that would never walk down the hall of one's life. It could be a long shift.

Double doors marked the boundary between the real world and their world. Two plexiglass windows scratched blurry by hopeless hands allowed patients to peer out and the outside world to peer in, permitting an exchange of glances barely inches apart, but light years distant. Each world saw itself as reality and subsequently feared the world on the other side. Those on the outside found themselves bracing fearful minds against the stark realization that insanity and mental bankruptcy, even in the best of circumstances, lurked only inches away. Those on the inside stared back through cavernous eyes that lived out the full horror of that truth, waiting for the arrival of sanity that, for most, would never come.

I passed through this door once when I began my shift, and again when I ended it. It was a step from one world into an entirely different one. And one day, Emily stood on the other side of that door with the thick plexiglass windows; lipstick smeared; hair in weak curls; a powder blue dress draped in loose folds over her emaciated body. Staring out from her world into the one outside, her eyes were set with irresistible anticipation and excitement. Deep blue pools reached out in profound longing, desperate in their desire to connect to something on the other side. Each day she would prepare herself, meticulously tending to her reflection in that faded mirror and then stand at those doors for hours – waiting – every day.

Curfew would come preciously at 10 o'clock. "But I know he's coming," she would say in a thin voice of surrender. "He said he would be coming!" Even in the throes of disappointment, she was resistant. Eventually we had to escort her away from the doors with the thick windows and guide her fragile frame off to a lonesome bed. Female staff members prepared her for yet another night of deep disappointment. Cries of the soul rose in muffled whimpers and glistening lines traced errant paths down cheeks made warm by the thin dusting of rosy blush. Her slight frame, wracked yet again by deep disappointment, would obediently roll into bed and draw itself into a tiny fetal position. Her grief had torn her down from the inside out, rendering her an aged infant who needed to be tucked into bed by staff members who, night after night, grieved along with her. In a few moments, she would drift off to sleep. Exhausted by pain, she would find some fleeting escape in slumber.

One unusually quiet night before my shift ended, I checked her room. Escorted by a female staff member, I paused over her bed. A thin wash of light lay tentative across the room, passively leaking from a night light, yellowed and weakened with age – just like Emily. Two thin blankets lay draped over a body worn thin by grief and the ceaseless lathe of disappointment. Shallow breaths punctuated by slight sighs told me that not even sleep was a sure escape. Lipstick, blush and thin curls drowned in disappointment mirrored a hopeful, yet hopeless, soul that found fitful sleep.

Next to her bed, cheap brass frames sported washed out photos of another distant time. In them, there stood a young woman who was strikingly beautiful and vivacious, clasping hands with a young man who himself was sturdy and robust. Caught by the faded images, I attempted to see Emily in those photos, to correlate the depleted woman in the bed with the bright and lively woman in the photo. It was fruitless. "That's her husband," my co-worker whispered in a tone laced with her own pain. And then there came a pause laden with the dread anticipation of what was about to be said. "He died in 1969."

I fell into an emotional rift, in the descent, slowly but persistently drawing together what I knew. Recognizing the devastation and hoping it not to be the truth I stammered and then asked, "Is that who she waits for?"

A muffled *yes* struck me. "She's done that every night for years." My mind raced to do the math that would provide me some measure of her pain so that I might identify with the suffering of this poor woman. She had been traveling to the door of disappointment for 13 long and lonely years.

Under my breath, I murmured what my heart was screaming, "She's waiting for someone who's never coming." Such a thought was the epitome of hopelessness: being unable not to hope, but hope always consumed by the futility of an eternally empty hallway. Hers was a truly hopeless life, for her hope was embedded in something that would never come. He would never walk down that hallway, and he would never peer through the thick plexiglass windows. Simply, he was not coming — ever.

Saturday

The void between what was and the hope that what had been might be restored was overwhelming. Both were encased in the unknown of a future that might yield neither. That void was accentuated by the sense that nothing might come, that the results of the painful events of the past might very well be what lay ahead. The "in-between" was neither what had been nor what would be, but was sheer anticipation rendered stalled in suspended animation. The disciples had experienced profound pain, loss, and personal devastation with no sign and no hopeful indication of restoration anywhere in sight. It was indeed a point in life where desperation seeped through the crevices of their hearts; saturated their souls; swept over their minds and suffocated their spirits – like Emily.

It was Saturday, although they hardly noticed it, if at all. The news had swept Jerusalem in a tidal wave of variant emotions that ranged from jubilation to devastation. The dam had burst. The disciples had thought it unthinkable. A sense of protection had surrounded Jesus, being so strong He had seemed entirely invincible. A week earlier the crowds had jubilantly heralded Him a conquering King, swirling around Him in a frenzy of disappointed and delayed messianic prophecy, with Jesus riding into Jerusalem in a blur of palm branches and praise. There was indeed an air of impregnability about it all. "The world has gone after him" (John 12:19) was an apt, albeit temporary, observation of the very ones who would soon find envy the foodstuff of murder and who would turn that same world against Him in the satisfying of that appetite.

Certain headiness had prevailed among Jesus' followers. A dozen simple Galileans had been swept up in something monumental, until it came crashing down at the very moment that kingship appeared consummated beyond rebuff. Suddenly and inexplicably, it fell with the thunder of heaven and the shaking of a shifting cosmos. A rush of impossible events would follow, somehow linking themselves together in a torrid race of wrenching and contrary emotions from Gethsemane to the cross and then to a borrowed tomb. The legalistic waters of religiosity and the territorial currents of politics had converged in a turbulent headwater on a barren hilltop. Flesh was shredded; blood was spattered; hate was seething; and spikes were driven. Jesus fell to it all, drawing a final breath as impossible and implausible as it seemed, and then was sealed in a tomb. And now, it was Saturday.

The reality had yet to sink in. Until it did, emotional paralysis dictated confusion, disorientation, and fear that fed and fueled even more paralysis. It was one of those places in life that everything upon which one has staked his life collapses, or so it seemed. Yet, nothing had fallen, for what appeared to collapse in their lives was little more than God making a hole of hopelessly impossible proportions so that the infinite God had enough elbow room to work a miracle. That's the stuff of God.

Scripture does not recount any events on the day between Jesus' death and His resurrection: 24 hours sandwiched between the two greatest events in history. Lost in the magnitude of them, John lived that day as did the other disciples, the women, the secret followers and God Himself. But those grueling 24 hours were that space between the known of past events and the unknown of those yet to occur; the abyss of uncertainty, where written history had yet to be balanced by that which was yet to be written. It was likely a time of not knowing if events were indeed an end in and of themselves or if they were a portent of something to come. The paralysis of that yesterday had left no room for speculation about tomorrow as trauma affords nothing other than trauma. Either way, when a life is in pain and turmoil, the unknown can be devastating. Such was Saturday.

We do not know where John and the others fled. The issue in fleeing is not the destination as much as it is the creating of distance between oneself and that from which one flees. Panic and fear too often equal flight away from what has elicited the panic and fear. But whatever the place they fled to, it was behind locked doors. Events on that first Easter morning would suggest they were assembled together at known locations, having stumbled into something with some familiarity when everything about them turned terribly unfamiliar. They apparently had not scattered or left the city.

It's likely that the disciples found hiding places, assuming one crucifixion might stir appetites for more. Waiting for the frenzy to wane sufficiently in order to slip out of the city, they likely contemplated a return to previous occupations because the blur of events left no room to contemplate anything other than that which they knew. The force of it all effectively sent them backward instead of forward, picking up old lives where they had left off as the path with Jesus had apparently terminated and trailed off at an empty tomb. In the turmoil, they did not recognize that God's beginnings are so massive they look like endings.

These three years of life and travel and astonishment with Jesus had been relegated to a diversion, a dream, and a wild hope murdered in a chilling compilation of beatings, jagged lacerations, torn cartilage, mangled tissue and blood. Blood had been everywhere: across His body, tracing thin rivets down rough-hewn timbers, splattering across the ground and across John's soul. A tornado of emotions had whipped a ravaging vortex across his life, both decimating and pulverizing three years with Jesus in a bloody instant. It raged in a funnel cloud that spun his mind in an unabated torrent, exchanging obedience to Jesus for obedience to fear. And so John sat, somewhere in Jerusalem, with the celebration of Passover filling and flooding the streets, not knowing what to do or think other than somehow try to do or think. He was abjectly mired in the dark of a lost soul that occurs when a friend dies who should not have died. No — a friend was murdered. And it was Saturday.

The Emptiness of My Saturday

Right now, it's Saturday for me. Another, far different Saturday than that experienced by John holed up somewhere in Jerusalem, or Emily in a psychiatric hospital, but the destructive and damaging events of the past are resonating within my mind. Mine is an emotional death, possibly the death of much more. However, I am not entirely sure because, for me, at this moment, this is Saturday. I'm between what was and what is yet to be, living squarely between a death of sorts and the unknown of the "What next?" It is my Saturday. If the "yet to be" is nothing more than what is transpiring right now, my future will be shrouded in the thick cold of bitter hopelessness. If it shifts ever so slightly, my future may be colored by the dark hues of personal devastation. A shift in a slightly different direction, and there may be jubilation.

But I don't know, for this is my Saturday, that "in-between" in which I have no alternative than to trust. I can feign control and attempt to alter circumstances toward a favorable outcome. I can go backwards to the last place where I felt safe and forfeit growth as a trade-off for comfort, but in my Saturdays, control is an illusion only, and I, like John, can only sit and hope. But hope for what?

Sunday ... The Day After
The sun had thrown only the first slight rays of light over the crest of the eastern horizon. It's that time that isn't quite night, but not yet morning, that "in-between." Mary had risen in the last blackness of the night, living the "in-between" of her own soul and of the day all at once. She wound her way through darkened streets; out the northwest gate; past the hill as fresh with memories as the blood that lay spattered on the ground; driven by the passion to provide her Lord the semblance of a proper burial to offset, in some small way, the horrific degradation of Friday and the deep dark of yesterday. If this were to be an end, she would make it an honorable one; bringing the best of her humanity together with whatever shred of faith had survived yesterday; walking through a still garden with that bit of humanity and faith symbolically wrapped in a bundle of cloth and spices. It was her offering for her Lord. She would not allow yesterday to be an end, at least not for her – not yet. She would be the first to see the inexplicable beginning rise from an impossible ending.

She felt her way down wandering paths through the dew-laden garden. The silence of the crisp morning seemed to mimic the forever silence of death. Her feet crunched as lone footsteps on the hard packed gravel. She remembered the tomb's location, having followed Joseph and Nicodemus there two days earlier. Rapid steps were marked with pensiveness as she stumbled, caught herself, and regained a tentative balance. Seeing His body would be fraught with terrible contradictions for her. She desperately desired to see Him once more. But seeing the corpse would only confirm the horrendous reality of His death, and it would cruelly validate the memories she had come to hope were but a terrible figment of her own imagination. Encountering God is always safe, but it always comes with great risk.

But something was different. Something was wrong and out of place. She turned a corner that was ever so slightly illuminated in the thinness of that first early light. Pausing, she turned her head slightly, squinted and stepped closer. The stone — had it been moved, or was the retreating darkness simply attempting to deceive her one final time before the light banished it? The morning light was tentative but sufficiently revealing. She drew closer, looked deep and confirmed that the stone had been moved, leaving the exposed entrance dark against morning's ascending light. Her natural assumption screamed through an already destitute soul: "The body had been stolen!"

She was suddenly panicked and doubly grieved. They killed Jesus, and now they'd stolen Him as well. In a rush of contradictory and confusing emotions, she ran madly to Peter and John, the chaos and pain of Saturday now seemingly minor compared to this cold thievery. Chaos seized her mind, hijacked her heart, and drove her amidst a torrent of tears that blurred streets and ran down flushed cheeks. A wild and panicked flight traced a stumbling course through the sleepy corridors and dozing alleys, each stride being punctuated by gasps for breath. Peter and John responded in kind, and a foot race back to the tomb ensued. Those who had roused early along the streets were puzzled by the activity, but it was lost in the larger mayhem of celebration.

John arrived first, entirely out of breath. Taking in the situation rather than rushing into it, he stepped up to the entrance, bent over slightly and peered in. Trauma rebelled against more traumas. His mind instinctively protected itself from more pain, and so he was pensive to believe his Lord was raised because there was great risk in finding it not to be so. The brash and bold demeanor of Peter found full expression as he arrived and ran into the tomb without pause or hesitation. Indeed, there was no body, but here life turned on one of those rare moments when we put ourselves before what appears lost and we allow ourselves to believe against all belief that God is not finished with what appears to be finished.

The grave clothes lay folded as if the use for which they were intended was of no value. Their purpose was finished and eternally completed. There was a torrential contradiction in it all, as death is irrevocably permanent — so are the grave clothes. But here all of this had been temporary, their purpose was concluded when there was supposed to be no conclusion.

They were folded and put away, relegated forever to the stuff of history. History presumes a future; otherwise, history is nothing more than an endless present. What was presumed as an end was not. Something entirely contrary to the natural order had transpired in the damp confines of the tomb, and it could not have happened without Saturday. Saturday was not an end, despite the completely convincing nature of the tomb. That afternoon He would appear to them. Indeed, Saturday was over.

God Holds Sunday

And that's how I try to live, not knowing what Sunday will hold, but knowing that God holds Sunday. The fact He holds Sunday assures its existence, and I can look forward to it from the dark confines of my Saturdays. If Sunday exists, it will come. What was dead and lost to me can be restored, whether that will occur soon or in the distant future, or possibly in the life yet to come, I don't know. But the "not knowing" of Saturday builds the faith necessary for the guaranteed "not yet" of Sunday to happen. A remarkable turn of events will mark the end of my Saturday and the beginning of a brand new day. And it is that hope that makes my Saturday bearable. That hope can even make the darkness and pain of my Saturday exciting, knowing that, with God, Saturday is only a causeway to Sunday. Sunday is always and only a sunrise away.

Goodnight Emily

Turning, I switched off the light in Emily's room and glanced back one final time. He was never coming. Yet, she was desperate for him to come. She had shaped her entire life around that hope, and she made it her sole reason for living, drawing from this single hope, a thin thread that gave her a reason to live in a reasonless life. But he wasn't coming – ever.

And so it is with so much of the world out there and the world we each have inside of us. Hopelessness pervades and consumes so many lives, like Emily's. But this sole hope we have: the assuredness that Jesus is coming back and that He will boldly stride down the long hallways of our lives. He will peer through the thick glass rendered foggy by hands that have constantly pressed it. He will throw wide the door and embrace us with an eternal embrace that wildly exceeds everything we hoped for, everything we dreamt that moment would be. He is coming, and Saturday will be over.

Craig D. Lounsbrough

Pondering Point

How hopeless is your life? Often life is dark, cold, foreboding — devastating even. And we wait for something that will never come, that will never be. We know it, but it's simply too painful to admit, and so we wait because not waiting admits to our souls that our hope will never arrive. But Jesus will come. He promises that "surely I am with you always, to the very end of the age" (Matthew 28:20 NIV). For the future, we have the assurance that "this same Jesus, who has been taken from you into heaven, will come back in the same way you have seen him go into heaven" (Acts 1:11 NIV). He will come at every point, in every place, at every time.

A Thought
- For what am I waiting?
- What have I pinned my hopes on?
- How desperate is my attachment to it?
- Do I live knowing Jesus Christ alone is the only sure thing that I can count on?

Chapter 15

Snowscapes of the Heart

The phone on my desk rang as it does many times each day. I reached for it, fumbled the receiver, and then picked it up. Habitually, I recited my customary greeting. On the other end, over a thousand miles away, death leapt into the receiver. Its gray fingers, frigid and experienced from the innumerable lives they had seized, thrust themselves through the miles of phone line. Leaping out of the receiver, they drew down into a fist that rammed all of its accumulated force into my heart.

I have emulated my father. As I grew and faced the complex realities of life, I would model his response as I had watched him face similar realities. He had always performed with a deft air of grace and ease, handling life as if it were feather light. It is only when I grappled with those same realities, and was more than once sent reeling by the intensity of their strength, that I realized how admirable my father's performance had been. How naive I had been to the steeled strength of the inner man that gave Dad the ability to be velvety soft on the outside and yet to forfeit absolutely nothing in life because of the underlying strength he possessed. I had no idea.

Death was, however, laying claim to this remarkable man. Like an advancing army, cancer had stormed the shores of his body. A beachhead had been established, and an advancing front followed a predictable, yet deadly, strategy. Stark x-rays bluntly mapped the invasion. Reams of test results analyzed the onslaught. Medical jargon sterilized death. The line of demarcation between life and eternity was abruptly erased, suddenly being redrawn nearly at his feet. Slipping into an emotional abyss, I dropped the phone. I slid down in my chair, stared out the window into the fiery reds and pungent oranges of a brisk fall day, and recognized that winter was coming – and coming quickly.

As with all the other battles that had unleashed themselves against him, Dad faced the news with grace and ease. With the receiver lifted back to my ear and with the hands of death now choking my heart, the grace and ease he exhibited eluded me. Once again his remarkable strength was evident even in death. Did he not understand the intent of the enemy or the ground seized? Could he not see that the first snowfall of his life was but a breath away? Had he taken refuge in the dullness of denial? I hung up the phone and cried.

That evening, I ascended the front porch of my home, each step infinitely weighed down by a heavy heart. Reaching for the door, I glanced over to notice my old sled leaning in one corner of the front porch, patiently awaiting winter's first snowfall. Halted, I turned, looked, stepped over to the old sled, and gently ran my fingers down its frame — and I remembered. Suddenly, I fell into a storehouse of memories embedded in its wood and metal frame. A horde of memories surged from over the hidden horizon of my mind and instantly overwhelmed me in a warm and wonderful blitzkrieg. An army of recollections stormed the beaches of my heart. They were all a liberating army, comrades every one of them, sweeping me off the porch and transporting me back in time to a different winter.

Suddenly I was there. The decades had melted as if they had never been. My father and I were careening down snow covered hills, soaring on numerous occasions and landing in places other than where the sled landed. We collided with trees that didn't move, and people who did, accumulating a lengthy list of assorted victims that included bushes, rabbits, other sleds and my father's '65 Dodge. Many a wild ride was abruptly terminated in ditches or snow banks at the base of innumerable hills. Lying prone, laughing as we dug impacted snow out of our coats and pants, we would look up and recount in precise detail the errant path down the snowy hillside that told of our kamikaze-style ride. Soon we were heading back to the top to do it all over again. Hot chocolate was dispensed, steaming from the old camping Thermos with dents that attested to its own journey. Cold hands clutched warm, frothy cups that steamed against the frigid winter chill. We quickly downed the thick, chocolaty sweetness to hit the hill again and again and again.

We were finally exhausted when, with the sun drawing down on a frozen western horizon dense with naked trees, the chill in the air would turn razor sharp. Dad would warm up the old Dodge, knock the accumulated snow off the sled, throw it into the trunk, and say, "Let's go eat!" And off we'd go, rambling into the twilight of a deep winter's day to a home-cooked meal whose delicious aroma would warmly greet us at the door. As I fell into mounds of thick blankets at bedtime, my young mind would again recount every wild and errant ride down those hills until exhaustion claimed me and lulled me off to sleep. Running trembling fingers across the sled, I realized the rides to the top of the hill were nearly over.

The Final Hill
This hilltop was not in mind for any of them. Sometimes life is so glorious and impossibly wonderful that the nature of it all excludes an end. It seems that some things were not meant to end as that would suggest: with a cruelty far too horrible to embrace. Something about whatever was transpiring should, by the virtue of its sheer wonder and goodness, go on indefinitely in order that the world might have the chance to romp in it forever. Such is the decadence and darkness of the world that beauty and wonder seem only able to offset it if they are given permission to always be — without end.

Joseph's own journey taught him all of that. His prominence had not skewed a greater sense of life. Neither had it narrowed him down to a rigid piousness that saw only self-serving agendas and messianic proclamations that could be controlled to one's favor. His heart remained supple and his eyes untainted. He saw in this Jesus something authentic that made any risk to retrieve the body entirely worth it. He pulled himself out of the delirium of the lost Messiah and headed to the Antonia towers. Stepping through the colonnades of marble, he moved ever farther into the lair of the very people who participated in the carnage he wished to take down from the cross. In such fashion, he went to Pilate in full societal view and requested the remnants of a dead man.

It was easier than he presumed. His request was granted. Perhaps Pilate was himself dealing with some element of grief, finding himself forced into an act of carnage that somewhere touched him. Maybe he simply wanted it over, the body sealed in the ground with all the political and religious intrigue sealed there as well. Proper protocol was followed: the ensuring of the death of this self-proclaimed Messiah. It was confirmed, and the request was granted. The empire moved on with other matters. Joseph quickened his stride and set out for a hilltop.

Bad, it seems, is temporal or at least should be. It dogs the good, existing only to thwart that which is pure and wholesome. It, therefore, rests on the good and finds its existence as a nemesis of that good. Should bad cease to exist, that good would likewise cease. Oddly, the very thing it seeks to destroy is the very thing that gives it reason for living. Good, however, has something timeless about it, something deep in the core of the created order that gives it an immutable centrality. It is so because it originates and rests in the heart of God Himself. It rolled around in Joseph's head as an attempt to reconcile that which cannot be reconciled.

The seeds of these ideas spun in the heads of the disciples as well. Their confluence only began in a death that was barely hours old. This assorted band of followers was sequestered in undisclosed locations in a celebrating city. The bond of their relationships forged over three years was groaning, tearing and at times, bringing comfort. The object of their devotion, the person whose life they cast everything away for and gave everything to lay cold on a vertical beam on a hilltop. It ended there. Theirs was a mix of confusion jaded with fear. Out of the traumatic details and events of the last day, little could be processed. Disorientation reigned, leaving little ability to intellectually climb out of the bottomless pit into which they had fallen. It was all paralysis. There was nothing else. They remained hidden.

In the sordid mix of it all, what was it like to take the body down? I wonder. The endeavor was impaled with risk and thick with the pillaging disappointment that spins confusion. It involved stepping up to claim the cold remains of the vanquished Messiah in full view of the adversaries who had created an embittered union to remove Him. Each of those parties sat in the solace of their separated palatial surroundings, digesting the effects of it all quite differently. The remnants of their shared venture still hung vertical on rugged beams, pasty with death and cold with pallor on a barren hilltop. It was over.

Joseph could not let it end that way. His was a mixture of allegiance and integrity that drew him to Pilate and then the hill. The death somehow had to be formalized so that it became real. Sometimes things have to be done so that the reality of the loss is verified. The body had to come down. It was the only right and respectable thing to do, and it forced the reality of the death into minds shrouded in denial.

It was up the hill with wraps, spices and all the dread of loss and fear of retaliation. It was down the hill carrying all of that in addition to a limp body drained of all the promise that He once held. The blur spun by a disoriented heart and traumatized mind rendered it all something surreal, a script of horror in which he unwillingly found himself. It was a weighty task, physically and emotionally. But His body had to come down from the hill one final time.

My Hill

The front porch and the sled ... I snapped back. The memories dissipated like an ascending vapor in a sympathetic breeze. I drew into the moment, and my head cleared. Staring at that old sled, I thought back over the many paths my father and I had made down the numerous hills of life. They were wonderful paths: full of fun, laughter, a dash of craziness, and a godly father.

Standing motionless, my eyes again welled with tears as I realized it was a path whose completion was close at hand. The trips to the top were nearly over: the wild rides, the legacy of memory and the greater legacy of life. With the frightening reality pounding my heart, I wiped the glistening lines from my cheeks and attempted to suppress the awful lump in my throat. And then I realized that, because God was afoot, Dad would also be afoot. Always. Cancer might take his body, but it could not take him. Out there, in the expanse of eternity, there is an infinite number of hills to be ridden, innumerable hills rising up in the landscape of eternity. There is an infinite amount of time to sled down each one, to create memories that will exceed those made in this life in ways unimaginable. Death on one hill granted me the possibility and hope of innumerable memories on a sea of hills in another place.

It is on the hills of eternity, if we can imagine them, that I will come to know my father in a manner so perfect and so comprehensive that it will be as if I had never known him at all. The sum of this life's memories are but the barest precursor that gives me only the faintest hint of what life with Dad will hold there. Such a thought frames death, it gives meaning to life as that preparatory moment in the breadth of eternity, and it implants impeccable hope. Hope in the face of phone calls and hills.

I laid both hands on the timeworn frame of the old sled, drew a staggered breath and said, "Thanks, Dad." Turning, I paused and uttered, "Thank You, God." Wiping away several final tears, I turned and opened the door, fully confident that Christ's work on one hill insures the preservation of all hills for all of eternity.

Pondering Point
We often frame our concept of life solely on the temporal nature we observe in this life, adopting a myopic sense of finality in lieu of a boundless sense of eternity, assuming that all of existence is marked by a fixed endpoint at which loss is irreparable. Embracing such an end because we cannot see beyond it, our inability to see the eternal evidences its lack of existence in our conceptualization of life. We succumb to the finite because we cannot grasp the magnitude of the infinite. And so, loss becomes permanent. And the permanence is devastating. It's devastating because life was not meant to be lived with the richness of living utterly lost. This renders the living implausible and meaningless because, despite all of its potential, it is doomed – doomed from the beginning. Life was meant to be cultivated here and then transferred to a place where it is forever celebrated and savored in all its beauty. Death, then, is not loss, but a step into the fullest manifestation of living: living shared forever.

A Thought
- Do I live with an eye on eternity, conceptualizing this life as a precursor to an existence where this life is fully and perfectly manifest?
- And if I do not, do I then strip this life of the wonder and anticipation that makes living everything it can be?

Chapter 16
The New Era

The first sunrise of the New Year had barely begun to stir the darkness. It arrived pensively, graced with a wisp of pastel pink in a thin wash on the eastern horizon. Barely visible to the eye, it reflectively traced distant hills. Tentatively set against the black of the receding night, it gently pressed a warming shoulder into the dark, nudging it westward. Slowly ascending the backside of the horizon, it peered over in mixed anticipation of what the New Year might bring. The air was cold and breathlessly still. The stars were silent, watching from aloft. Nature was holding its breath.

The sun, gentle but steady, slightly widened the thin wash of pastel pink and edged it with splashes of powdery peach, mauves and pools of soft gold. Oaks and maples, silhouetted as silent sentries, submitted to the greater miracle of the earth turning its face toward the sun. Darkness still prevailed, but found itself being rubbed warm into ever lighter hues of sky blue as the earth rolled over into another day. The lone sound of my footsteps on loose gravel was free from the inhibitions of other sounds that might have diminished it. The leash pulled, and we ventured out into the first light of that New Year. They were steps taken into a new era.

A New Era
Scripture does not recount Jesus walking out of the tomb or those moments just before that event; an obvious intended omission. That moment was left for speculation, possibly being even too sacred for Scripture itself. Maybe it was a moment exclusively for Jesus, that moment He had anticipated from eternity past that only He could see through to an eternal conclusion that morning. Maybe it was not to be intruded upon, possibly left for

simple wonderment, the mystery of the moment stirring speculation in those who would ponder it for countless centuries. Nonetheless, I can't help but wonder.

Three gardens. The task was destined from eternity past and proclaimed in a perfect garden that fell to a serpent's deception. The fall was grieved with incarnate angst in a second garden. Redemption was secured forever in the third. The satanic rebellion had been quelled, the din of battle having rolled into the annuals of history and proclaimed eternally as God's victory. Peace was restored. Angels seized the stone and effortlessly rolled it aside. The final obstacle was removed. The tomb was unsealed. Victory ... sealed.

With the stone removed, cool morning air drifted into the tomb, challenging the damp air of death and the proclamation of finality that death had, until that moment, held unchallenged. Death was subjected to an impossible experience that even it could not comprehend, having been diluted and then dissipated. The fresh air was drawn deeply into His lungs. He held it for a moment in silent triumph and then exhaled. He emptied air breathed by lungs once dead, the first time since His last breath three days earlier. His lungs drew in another breath, expanding and finding their rhythm. It was as it had been at that Bethlehem manger. The cycle was complete. He shifted, rotated and then sat erect. God was arising.

His hands reflectively emerged from the deep folds of His funeral wraps. The calluses of a carpenter were deep and thick, the broad hands of legacy. They were strong hands that shaped wood, shaped lives, and shaped history by being nailed to wood. His hands drove sickness out of weary bodies; brought light to blind eyes; ran across the gross disfigurement left by leprosy; beckoned a disciple to tread on the waves; and clawed the soil in Gethsemane. They bore the marks of crucifixion, without which, this second genesis moment would be impossible.

It is indeed the scars in incarnated flesh that draw the deepest reflection. Spikes had been driven with blows weighted by the sins of all mankind: combined, focused and distilled into each fall of the mallet. The cross had been lifted with every sin pressing as gravity and sin seized the elevated body in tandem. The grief, horror, hatred, selfishness, and fear of a thousand generations were all pressing down at one terrible moment.

Every tear. Every incident of abuse. Every lie. Every murder. Every shred of depression. Every moment of frustration. All of the shame and desperation sustained by a thousand generations and more. Every ounce of it, every drop, ran salty, burning fiery like His sweat, into wounds of ripped flesh. A billion faces flashed before Him. A hundred billion tears came with them. Cries, moans ... the bruised and brutalized voices of the past, those seized in pain at that moment and those yet to cry. All of them were there. All of them were loved. Their pain was now His, the immensity of it all obliterating the pain of torn flesh and spikes. "My God ..." But standing in the tomb, it was over -- forever.

He drew Himself into a standing position, thoughtfully scanned the rock walls, and then shifted His gaze outside. Herein was the new dichotomy of living where death takes life and inters it but is forced to surrender it back again. Death, the great thief, must relinquish its captive to a life from which that life can never again be stolen. Death's hands were rendered slippery and arthritic, unable to hold that which it seized, despite how much it might tighten its grip. Life was but a step away from whatever death might do. And so He shifted His gaze outside.

A wisp of pastel pink in a thin wash on the eastern horizon greeted the planet rolling itself over into the new day. It is indeed over, He whispered. "It is finished." He drew deeply into the moment. The people walking in darkness have seen a great light; on those living in the land of the shadow of death a light has dawned (Isaiah 9:2 NIV). Indeed, the sunrise on this single morning hailed the dawning of an infinitely larger light, the promise of a dawn of ever increasing degrees of light that dispel the darkness by allowing it no room. It was perfect. He uttered a word of profound thanks to His Father, drew into Himself the totality of what that moment meant, and smiled.

History would pivot on His next step. The hopes of millions now dead would, in those next steps, see their hopes finally fulfilled. The hope of billions unborn would rest squarely on that moment. Creation had paused before. It had gasped awestruck in the face of God's works many times as He had lived large enough to fling entire galaxies into space and yet be small enough to comfort crying children and touch grieving widows. But no moment was like that one. For there, and there alone, mankind was redeemed and creation was released. It was not about creating as much as it was about recreating by releasing the creation. All that was before and all that would follow would draw its life, its sustenance, its hope from that single moment.

Angels waited outside. They were sentries at the first garden with flaming swords, once drawn to keep sinful man out of that which he desired to return to after realizing too late the devastation of deception. The sentries were now at a very different garden that would invite man back: God's redemption coming full circle. They had heralded His birth to shepherds in distant fields. They had knelt at His side after 40 days of fasting, and they had restored Him. Only a few days before, they stood beside a lone figure in the garden, wiping great drops of blood from His brow; His disciples were asleep not far away. The next day, they had stood on tiptoe, awaiting His command to surge forth and save Him from His own execution. He never summoned them. The spikes were driven, and the cross was raised. The words My God, why have you forsaken me? deafened them as they pounded the cosmos and sent a violent tremor through the halls of heaven. And the whole of the angelic host fell deathly silent as His last shallow breath was drawn and His body went limp. The intensity of their grief darkened the sky and shook the earth itself.

And now, in sentinel formation, they stood outside the tomb in reverent but wild anticipation of that next step. Jesus paused, His mind on the millions past and the billions to come. Creation was frozen and breathless. He drew His cloak around Himself, ran His fingers across the cold stone one final time — and then He stepped from death's grip.

The sun, gentle but steady, slightly widened the thin wash of pastel pink and edged it with powdery peaches, mauves and pools of soft gold. Oaks and maples, silhouetted as silent sentries. Darkness still prevailed, but was being rubbed warm into ever lighter hues of sky blue. The lone sound of His footsteps on loose gravel was free from the inhibitions of other sounds that might diminish it. The moment pulled Him, and He ventured into the first light of this new era. Heaven erupted in thunderous applause. The angels, lost in this final victory, bowed in deep and victorious reverence, witnesses of the steps across the millennia that culminated in that single step.

Shortly, He would meet the women. They would be the first to know.

Already emotionally conflicted by the pronouncement of the angels, they were waiting in angst. He appeared incognito on the road to Emmaus. Then, it was off to Galilee: home. Then, he was off to the Sea of Galilee with another great catch of fish just like one three years prior, to a disciple needing to be restored over breakfast. What fun! Implausible reunions with doubting disciples wrapped in 40 days and 500 encounters. And then His real home at the right hand of His heavenly Father. It had begun.

The cosmos exhaled. Heaven shook again, but it was the exhilaration of victory raised in thunderous applause, not the tremor of defeat. If God cannot defeat death, He cannot be God anyplace else. The tomb is indeed empty. Death is defeated. It is a new era.

Embracing the New Era
A golden crescent bared a flaming edge and emerged from the womb of the earth. The sun peaked the expanse of the horizon. The wisp of pastel pink in a thin wash on the eastern horizon deluged the sky in a flood of deep peach, mauve and glistening gold. I turned toward home. The birds began to stir, energized by the first light, building to a raucous melody of simple joy, high in lofty limbs. Squirrels darted about through the loamy leaf litter piled in the underbrush and scampered effortlessly up sturdy limbs. A slight breeze brushed my face. Nature awakened to a new year. It was already promising, ushered onto the stage of eternity as only God could do it, as only Jesus could do it on that day when He ushered in a new era.

Pondering Point
In the flow and facts of life, we often feel entombed. We're constricted and constrained by forces and realities both within and without, by situations rendering life little more than a living death. And we sense no escape. We see no door, no point of exit, no way by which we are able to elude the confinement. And here, life closes down, devolving into futility. It shackles us with steeled chains of abject hopelessness. Of our own devices, escape has been futile. Hope has been disappointed so often that we refuse to hope. "The risk of hope deferred" (Proverbs 13:12 NIV), is too poignant and too painful. Such a realization forces us to likewise embrace our imprisonment. And if it is embraced, life turns intolerable. In all this, it is realizing that Jesus walked out of a far greater tomb; all our tombs are far inferior to that one. If He walked out of His tomb, He can likewise walk us

out of ours. And He extends just such an offer.

A Thought
- Have I surrendered to my tomb?

- If I have, am I willing to risk believing one more time that freedom is possible?

- If so, am I willing to ask Jesus to roll away the stone and walk me out into the dawn of an exhilarating new day?

Chapter 17

How Very Many Years

Pearl Harbor was yet to be strewn with twisted steel and bloody memories. The bombs would fall only seven months later, listing the Arizona and littering the glistening Pacific harbor with wreckage of both metal and flesh. Tommy Dorsey and Glenn Miller were setting the cadence for a golden generation that was about to draw itself up from the commitment to isolationism and hurl itself against beaches from Guam to Normandy. The Depression was itself dwindling, as fixed eyes, still burning from the acrid smoke of Pearl Harbor, scanned both Europe and the South Pacific.

In May of 1941, he passed out of life, long before I entered it. There was no loss in that, I was told. The sordid stories that had drifted down the foggy decades told of a man of rage, alcohol and smoky pool halls. He had been a saxophone player with an artistic soul, gradually suffocated by life and drowned in the liquid abyss of alcohol. The notes had soured. His heart had stopped long before the heart attack. His shadow had vanished from the doorpost when my father was a tender six, leaving a wife and four children to face the destitution of the soup lines, raging unemployment and a nation adrift.

For my father, the loss was inexplicable, slicing deep. A young heart yearning for a father in the very vacancy of a father, irresistibly drew six-year-old feet in worn shoes down dusty alleys to the derelict pool hall his father had traded for his family. Peering through glass smeared by filth and yellowed by smoke, his eyes cautiously searched the vagrant mix of alcoholics and wayward men who sat about in smoky stupors. The sharp crack of billiard balls, muffled conversation and clanking glasses drifted through dense layers of smoke that saturated the room. A six-year-old heart searched the sordid array of drifting humanity, hoping to catch a fleeting glance of a father who would never come home. Eventually, catching a glimpse of this errant child, his father would glance over furrowed brows and callously shout, "What do want, boy?" The snickers of assorted pool hall vagrants in the throes of inebriation added their own caustic smoke to the thick air surrounding youthful innocence. A bloodied heart that caused the boy to press hopeful eyes against a pool hall window would find itself rewounded yet again by a calloused father.

The need to run would seize him, even though the pain was so overwhelming that determining where to run was, at that moment, impossible. Sometimes the running away leaves no room to determine what or where we are running to. Such was that moment. Tears, profuse and blinding, wet and searing, would fall without restraint. Wiping them with worn sleeves as he dashed around dusty corners of vacant streets, he would finally scurry under the weatherworn front porch where he would attempt to seek solace that no porch could ever afford him. His was a deep depression in the Great Depression.

But time passed. Then the death of his father arrived, and a sullen burial simultaneously embraced both pleasure that he was gone and grief that any hopes of a father were dashed. Seven brief months later, Pearl Harbor erupted and men marched off to war. At 19, my father went off to serve. Eventually the Axis fell, and America got back to the business of home and hearth. The decades rolled by in a blur of marriage, children, family and everything from which the tapestry of life is woven. As it is with life, 1999 rushed onto the stage, leaving us wondering where the other years had gone.

My grandfather was an anomaly to me. A few tokens and shards of various stories were mere pieces of a puzzle that, when put together, provided only the vaguest representation of whoever it was that he had been. A single black and white photograph, stained by time and discolored with mottled edges, gave the mystery more intrigue. It had been taken before his innocence and giftedness were offered up to the gods of alcohol and narcissism. His face was filled with promise not yet stolen. All the things he could have been were still there to be realized.

There was his pocket watch, gold and bejeweled. It was, in many ways, what he had been, but was never to be. Then there were the other stories: abuse, drunken rages and litanies of caustic verbal barrages that sent emotional shrapnel ripping through whomever they were directed at. The recollections were shadowy, coming to me out of the haunting grayness of an era long gone. It was all a misty appendage of my history that possessed too little firmness to take hold of. It was my life, that from which I descended.

And so it was in 1999 that I visited home. My father was 76. The death of his father loomed 58 deep years in the past. Yet, inside my father was a six-year-old boy who carried the pain of smoky pool halls and the cobwebs strewn on the underside of creaky front porches. He had never visited his father's grave. There was yet the pain of simply finding himself unable to draw up enough compassion to nudge him there; to the granite edifice that marked the place he had stood as his father was lowered into the soft spring soil seven months before a December bombing half a world away; the place from which he would depart into World War II and then into life. "I want to go see Grandpa," I said.

My father paused and then leaned back into the folds of the recliner. Passively, he eyed me and then cast wandering glances across the floor. Sometimes you can hear pain in total silence, and I heard it. "You don't have to go," I said. "But I want to ask your permission to go. I don't want to resurrect any pain for you, but I'd like to see the grave."

For the briefest of moments, he went back. The assorted memories drew themselves up from across the misty decades etched in his soul. They raced, it seemed, across the forefront of his mind. A myriad of emotions reintroduced themselves to him in the blur of a handful of seconds and thrust him back into his chair. Pictures and snapshots taken by a six-year-old heart flashed across a 76-year-old mind, instantly coalescing into that place and that time. For a moment, the decades vanished and he was back in pool halls and under front porches. I grieved that I had broached the subject at all. His pain was far in excess of any selfish need I had to piece together my past. Quietly, he leaned forward, collected a few words, and once collected, he turned and said, "I think it's time I went."

Fifty-eight years changes things. The cemetery looked different, far different from that day in May of 1941. Several circuitous drives around the cemetery yielded no recollection of where the grave might be. No familiar landmarks protruded from a changed landscape. The mystery of his burial was as thick as that of his life. Stopping at the cemetery office, we secured a plot map designating where he lay. It was a map to the man of mystery. Navigating the thin, winding roads, a landmark finally leapt out from the oblivion of a grave lost. "I recognize that oak tree," Dad muttered. "He's there, by that oak. I remember that."

The car rolled up a slight gravel berm. The sound of crunching gravel slowed and then stopped. Suddenly, time vanished. It was again May, 1941. My father paused, fumbled to put the keys away, and reached for the car door. We stepped out into another May day just like that one 58 years earlier. And then the memories rolled in a torrential deluge, bringing with them those long forgotten. Recalling tombstones adjacent to his father's, my Dad worked his way to his own father across the resting places of other distant relatives – and the resting places of his own pain buried deep in the plot of his heart.

There was a tension in his heart, I think. The desire to quickly find the grave and deal with whatever emotions it was to bring. This was wed with the equally powerful desire to keep his father deep in his own past where he could not reach into the present. Emotional meandering grew as he stepped closer to the grave. "Here it is," my father said. And silence fell. Fifty-eight years suddenly surged and truncated in that single moment. He knelt and brushed back the grass that had grown around the headstone, wanting, it seemed, to reach out and love his Dad. Then, ever so gently, he ran his fingers across the name engraved in the cool granite and down past the date. Trembling fingers dropped to his side, reflecting a moment in which no one could join him. Tears welled in the corner of eyes softened by the years. "I should have come before," he said. "I waited too long ... I waited too long."

How Many Days

"... what must I do to inherit eternal life?" (Mark 10:17 NIV) His riches had not waived off the question. His acquired assets had not insulated him. Wealth was not a guarantor either for eternal life or against the inevitability of death. It left the most fundamental issue of life abjectly untouched and unaltered. Earthly power was stifled and stymied when it came to matters of eternity. The various trappings of power, prestige, wealth and wisdom were useless, a preponderance of illusions that wielded nothing other than the illusion itself. And there he was. Wealth kneeling and power prostrate before God disguised as an itinerant preacher out of Nazareth, he asked about the one thing that exceeded his grasp and laid far outside his sphere of influence. "... what must I do to inherit eternal life?"

The children had only begun to disperse when the rich young man approached. It had been a lesson in simplicity. "...anyone who will not receive the kingdom of God like a little child will never enter it" (Mark 10:15 NIV). Could it be that simple? Could all that God is and wants be distilled down to that? Is that not the wonder of the infinite? The ability of that which has no end to pack all its vastness into the simplicity manifest in the life of a child? Only God could do that. And in the apprehending of that fact, eternity is revealed for the simplest of us to see. No wealth. No power. Not wisdom. Not prestige. Access to God is the absence of earthly resources or means obtainable by men. It is pure faith, the sole and single nard of heaven, grasped by eyes unspoiled and untainted by the allures of life. It is the unsullied windows of souls untarnished, not yet caught in the vice grip of works, achievements, successes and meritorious efforts, that purchase what only God can give. It's all the abject futility of the finite attempting to purchase the infinite, in and of itself an irreconcilable exchange rate. The task is to reclaim the eyes of a child when adulthood has hazed them foggy and thick with the mist of life.

He was resplendent, draped in thick chains of gold and silver. He wore deep fabrics dyed in the richest of bedazzling colors bespeaking their cost. Wraps of silk edged in decorative threads wound themselves lightly around his frame. Perfumes laced the air with thin and buoyant aromas of distant lands. The nard of earth was lavished on him, rendering his skin soft, supple and clear. Rings wrapped long fingers in variant jewels set deep in settings of precious metals that caught bits of sunlight and effortlessly threw them in a dazzling dance of golden light.

His entourage surrounded him, servants adept and poised to meet every need. The laughter of dispersing children was fading into the background. It was simplicity brushing up against complexity for a brief moment, skipping off in the joy and abandon that riches and power had found elusive.

They were so elusive they sought this impoverished Nazarene. In the end, it would be simplicity and simplicity alone that would have been able to grasp this Savior. Faith meeting fortune; innocence meeting influence; in it, all power meeting perfection. The fading sounds of children embodied that for which this rich young man sought, but even though it was so very close, it would elude him. That for which he knelt was within earshot, little more than a decision of surrender away. But he would not, he could not, grasp it.

A bronze Galilean stood before Him. There was nothing of earth's manufactured magnificence in Him. "He had no beauty or majesty to attract us to him, nothing in his appearance that we should desire him" (Isaiah 53:2 NIV). Weathered with calloused hands broad and strong, feet dusty and worn from walking the long and arduous back roads of man's pain. His eyes were set soft with a hint of the eternal lying deep in a slight sparkle. Discerning, His eyes cut through the self-placating decor the young man had wrapped his life in. Riches and power had coalesced in an unseasoned mind, unable to balance their weight and passion. Moreover, he had come seeking a twofold existence, acquiring and holding the treasures of earth and the treasures of heaven in a joint venture that would secure him both. He was voraciously seeking to find an answer that would permit his privilege and gain God's graces. Such a posture relieves us of choice and allows us to avoid commitment, for commitment to everything is commitment to nothing.

The sound of children had faded; innocence wafted off on a slight breeze that ruffled the folds of Jesus' robe. Jesus paused and then scanned the attendants. His gaze shifted to the young man. Drawing a firm and confident breath, He said, "You know the commandments: 'Do not murder, do not commit adultery, do not steal, do not give false testimony, do not defraud, honor your father and mother" (Mark 10:19 NIV). Legalism could answer in the affirmative and it did. It seemed, for the briefest of moments, the rich young ruler had achieved his goal and had been granted permission to live out his life commitment to both worlds – nothing lost. Such is the goal of man: to live life as a buffet from which he can make his assorted choices and have each affirmed as congruent with all others. In this manner, we are never put in a position of having to deny ourselves or become subservient to anything other than our own passions.

'Teacher,' he declared, 'all these I have kept since I was a boy' (Mark 10:20 NIV). At that point, God was everything this young man wanted Him to be. Nothing had to die. There would be no graves to visit, for nothing would need to be buried. He paused, and then began to stand, assuming that all had been said.

Jesus stared long, feeling a love for this young man commensurate with the young man's misdirected love for his own wealth. And then the words fell. 'One thing you lack,' he said, 'Go, sell everything you have and give to the poor, and you will have treasure in heaven. Then come, follow me' (Mark 10:21 NIV).

It did not happen. The power of this world's hold and its rationale was too much. He was too deep in the world to become deep in God, for you cannot be deep in both.

Scripture never again mentions this young man. We do not know where his life went from that moment. Apparently, it did not intersect Jesus or the disciples from that point forward. We can assume this encounter rolled through his mind many times in the years that followed. How many times had he forced the memory out of his head so that it would not impede his efforts to secure additional wealth or extend the scope of his influence in political affairs? How many times did he go to the temple, but find it empty because legalistic religion had not been enough that day so long ago? And because of that, how many times did he attempt to force a contrived religion that would somehow surpass or invalidate what Jesus had told him? How many times did he see a poor person on some dusty street corner and find himself back at the feet of Jesus? And how many times did he throw a few coins in their direction, hoping that somehow compromise would suffice both to please God and soothe his own disrupted conscience? For how many years did he fight the existence of that moment and, by virtue of that, forfeit the very living he sought?

Most importantly, how many times did it dawn on him that he died the day he refused to follow Jesus' commands and that no amount of money or power could ever resurrect him? Did he realize that, without facing death, he was merely existing under the guise of living? I wonder if he ever visited that grave before his physical death. Did he go back in order to go forward? If he had, he would have lived.

Within 10 minutes, we strolled leisurely back to the car. Ten minutes had apparently been enough. Ten minutes altered 58 years. He went back, and because he did, he could go forward. Dad's step was lighter; his affect clearer; his eyes were somehow sharper. Dropping into the driver's seat and adjusting his seatbelt, he put the key in the ignition and then dropped both hands into his lap. Turning toward me, he paused to again collect his words, tilted his head a bit and said, "Thanks for thinking of this." What had been buried in him for almost six decades was no longer buried. And he was different because of it. He was alive.

Pondering Point
There are things that we bury because we prefer them buried. Somehow, we feel that both they and we are better off in that state. But that is often not the case. Living means connecting with what we've buried because we have not resolved whatever that death meant for us. Whether that is a person, a belief, a choice, it matters little. These things may die, but they are not necessarily dead. They are truly dead when we bring ourselves back to what we refused to bring to closure and deal with it, as did my father.

Thoughts
- For how many years have we buried something and refused to return to it?
- How many?
- And what are those things that we refuse to go back to?

Chapter 18
The Miner's Hut

It was not possible – or so it seemed. She had always been old as held to the standards of a pimple-faced teenager. This was much the same. Tattered edges attested to the repeated handling by the hands of time. Black and white, its images were flat. Time frozen, it was a window to another era. I desperately wished I could step through it into the scene just as the camera had snapped the picture, at the very point where the participants relinquished their rigid poses and resumed their work. Have it happen right then. Erase the 70 years between the movement of that shutter, the capturing of the image on the film, and the moment in which I stood.

She was but 12 years of age. Long pigtails hung down over half the length of her petite frame. A slight smile betrayed the rigidity of posing for the camera. Her siblings and parents stood round about her in front of a clapboard farmhouse that was already aged by time, its sweeping front porch slightly canted. Rough-hewn wooden shingles, dried and warped, seemed scattered across the roof. A window was ajar, tentatively tilted in its frame. A split rail fence framed a never-ending sea of crops beyond. Chickens, having wandered into the photo, seemed not as distractions, but as much a part of life as the people posing there. It somehow felt barren.

I glanced up from the picture into the soft, deeply wrinkled face of my grandmother, furrowed lines etching her history across her brow, chronicling the vast sweep of time between the photo and that moment. Her hair was now washed white with time. The unmistakable musty scent of age proliferated. Wrinkled hands with palms worn smooth from the decades of labor yet ahead of the girl with the pigtails trembled slightly

— uncontrollably. Tears drew up in the corners of weakened eyes, seeped through deep crevices and traced thin lines down her mottled cheeks. "I remember when they took that picture," she said. I could not correlate the face before me with the one in the photo. They could not be one in the same. Time's work could not be so powerful as to change someone so completely. Could time indeed be that transforming?

The Irrepressible Flow of Time

Time – its march toward the next minute is insatiable, always toward the next minute, the next hour, the next day or decade or century. But its incessant cadence is likewise transforming. It is unable, or unwilling, to leave this moment the same in the next. This thin slice of time that marks the present moment irreversibly cascades into the past in an unstoppable torrent of time. On the other end of it, the future spills into the present through floodgates that are frozen open. And so we live in this wild raging river of time. We cannot dam it. Divert it. Force it to pool in some reservoir long enough to savor life a little more fully, to hold the beauty of a moment longer than simply a moment. We're unable to cherish what we have and who we have without watching them helplessly slip through our fingers.

Lost in her own history, my grandmother's trembling fingers softly ran across the black and white image on the faded photograph. Cherishing what time had taken. Wishing she could go back and apply the lessons of time she had not had when the camera snapped the picture that day. Hearkening back past Vietnam; crossing over the phenomena of the 50s; back beyond Korea; passing over Pearl Harbor; the Depression and dough boys marching off to face the Kaiser in a moonscape of trench warfare. It was before the model T, radio, and the miracle of flight achieved by the Wright brothers on a blustery Carolina beach. She went all the way back to her roots, back to the 12-year-old girl in the picture.

She sighed, dabbed tear-stained cheeks and collected herself. Clearing her throat, she lay down the photo, pressed a weathered hand against it one more time and turned. "I want to show you something." Reaching deep into a chest full of time-worn mementos, she pulled out a thin volume. Its binding was frayed, the cover slightly tattered. Yet, legible on its mottled surface were the words *The Miner's Hut*. Carefully, she opened it and gently turned the first few pages. Again, she went back across time, but even further back, to something immeasurably more powerful than even the photo. Closing the book, she pressed it between her hands and then held it to her chest as one would something indefinably precious. Suddenly, two trembling hands held it out to me. "This was my textbook from first grade."

How do you hold something so sacred? How do you handle the past of another? She laid it in my hands. And with it fell the weight of her history. Leaning back in her chair, she peered at me with soft eyes and said, "I want you to have it." Tears welled up in my eyes. I paused. In disbelief, I gently opened it. On the first page, there were three words. They were written in pencil by young hands that were yet unfamiliar with words. They revealed hands and a heart groping to learn. There were the words "cat, rat, mat." They were but the scribbling of a child sitting in a drafty one-room schoolhouse at the end of the 19th century, long before the events of the 20th century had even begun to unfold. I turned another page – the copyright date: 1870. The book marked the era of her father who lived as a Civil War veteran, a pioneer and farmer, scratching a living out of the soils of Ohio. My mind then leapt across two generations to that of my great-grandfather. Suddenly I was something more: a part of those who had gone before me. The whole moment seemed to create a vehicle where I was carrying them within me, bringing to this generation the foundation they had laid in theirs. It was a gift to carry, a baton to pass along.

As I write this, the book is sitting before me, calling out to me in silence. The voices of those gone before echo across the rifts of time and rise from its weary pages. Granny died in 1985. She wanted to be buried in the shade of a spreading oak. And so she was. Her gift to me: immeasurable. Her legacy: immutable. Her memory: precious. It lives today — right now.

Permanency

The breeze subtly drew gentle fingers through the folds of His cloak. A soft cascade of golden rain poured from a blue sky. It traced His features and rolled off to inundate the hillside. Thick grasses waved in unison in a waltz with the tepid breeze. Birds darted in a dance of frenzied flight. The soft drone of lumbering bees lent a gentle hum of satisfaction. Wisps of white charted unknown paths across the ocean blue sky. Sweet scents of tender grasses and buoyant wildflowers blended in a warm aroma. It was all a tantalizing wisp of heaven slipping over into this world as He did, brushing across their faces, brushing across His.

Craig D. Lounsbrough

The Eleven stared and exchanged blank glances with each other. Their minds were unable to grasp it all, to draw it in and accept it as real. Again and again, they stared, the eyes of the soul squinting to apprehend what logic would not allow. They saw Him die. From life to death, that is a familiar and expected journey. But leaping back across an endless chasm from death to life? That was incomprehensible. His eyes and His voice, the mannerisms and gestures forever gone were forever back. That bearded smile was so full. It was all there. But the additions, the scars of brutality, were new. They spoke as a testament to the instruments of death, the journey to death – and the return from death.

Three years of relationship, of journey that was poignant and painful, precious and profound, had irrevocably terminated on a cross. It was over and settled, having spilt over the precipice of time deep into the chasm of history. It was a chapter closed; the disciples had begun to settle into the unwanted reality. They had begun the arduous process of shifting through reams of emotions and trauma and lost hopes and shattered imaginings. But now He was back, and all of that somehow needed a new place.

And then, the immutable words that surged across that hillside deeply resonated as I read them and wrote them here; reclaiming my relationship with Granny and all who have gone before. Wonderful words of promise! "And surely I am with you always, to the very end of the age" (Matthew 28:20 NIV). Is that not the security we yearn for? The oddity of the toll of time is that relationship feels as if it should be permanent. It should be something that isn't to be lost or to succumb to the defiant river of time. Pain in loss of relationship is, I think, related to the deeply fundamental sense that relationships should not be simply for a time or a moment – or even an era. Something essential and deeply central to our core cries out for the rightness of permanence. Relationships should have something of the indefinite about them, something eternal even.

"He has made everything beautiful in its time. He has also set eternity in the hearts of men" (Ecclesiastes 3:11 NIV). Time creates beauty. It shapes, molds, matures and refines everything toward the infinite reflection from which it has fallen. Its brush paints lavishly beautiful strokes across the canvas of our lives. It adds rich chapters to our volumes. It relentlessly weaves richly colored threads into an ever deepening and widening tapestry. Such things are not meant to be achieved and then lost. Gained and then forfeited. Built and then destroyed. There is nothing of the eternal in that.

The grief is found in the wrenching incongruence that what is supposed to go on does not. What should be lasting is fleeting. What has been painstakingly crafted with the currency of years and pain into a rich and promising foundation that holds ever-increasing promise is robbed of the very promise through its demise. There is something wrong and unjust in it all, suggesting permanence.

This awful gnawing reality grinds against something inherently deep within us, something that cries out in the devastation of loss that should not be. Why? From where does that come? It arises from the small kernel of eternity that has been set in the hearts of men. Dulled by sin; yes. Muted by unbelief; absolutely. Rent and torn by our self-centered wanderings; without a doubt. Suffocated to near death by personal extravagance and arrogant defiance of God; we would be remiss to think otherwise. But it is there nonetheless. All of our power and assorted actions cannot kill it. Diminished, it still calls with a pervasive voice that we cannot silence. It still infiltrates our deepest selves and will not allow us to relinquish the eternal. And when a relationship ends in death, our inability to reconcile a loss in the face of permanence elicits wrenching grief. What is not supposed to be is.

"And surely I am with you always, to the very end of the age" (Matthew 28:20 NIV). What sin terminated, Jesus restored, reconciling that sense of permanence. He handed back to us the assurance that what appears to end here is only a continuation of something in eternity. So fabulous is life and all that makes up life, it could not possibly end as the river of time terminates into the lake of death. The lake of death is the reservoir of eternity. Life is far too complex and far too expansive to be held in the tiny pool of years that we have. It is profoundly detailed and fundamentally intricate in ways beyond human comprehensive and termination. Life screams of the eternal. It shouts it, celebrates it, and reflects it in the depth of the human spirit and the wildness of a cosmos unrestrained by an end. And Jesus promises it in the fundamental relationship we have with Him.

A Reminder That We Have Just Begun
The Miner's Hut is only a reminder. It is not simply or solely a reminder

of something that allows me to hold onto something I lost in defiance of the loss. Rather, it is a harbinger of what is yet to come, a reminder that the grave is not a sullen termination as much as the finality of death suggests. It is a declaration of a life lived and a promise of the resumption of that life. It is not a reminder of the past as much as a declaration of that life fully manifest in the future, recollection, and a hope seamlessly interwoven. Indeed *The Miner's Hut* is a reminder that one day she will again hold my hand, speak in soft tones, show me the photos, and tell me the stories. And for that, I can't wait.

Pondering Point
We hold to many evidences and reminders of our past. Treasures and trinkets alike. A myriad array of memories and mementos. In these, we can embrace and celebrate our assorted histories. But we can also view them as a reminder that those lives and those histories will be fully manifest and made perfect in eternity. There, what we hold in our hands will be celebrated with an incomprehensible fullness, being all they could never have been in this life. And so, as we hold to our past, may we see it as a promise and portent of our future, a glorious continuation of all the wonder and beauty extolled by our histories. May it be a flagrant display of all we've come from and all time has taken from us, manifest in stunning perfection.

A Thought
- How would my understanding of life be different if I saw eternity as the full and perfected manifestation of my past?
- How would I view my life if all that was good in my history were brought to fullness and I was allowed to live in its perfection forever?

Chapter 19

Seventy Cents of Simplicity

He was four-years-old — barely. He had a boyish innocence that was tightly stitched, and he held fast to a deep zest for living. He was a mosaic of the threads of a splendid tapestry whose fibers were being woven into a soft spirit that reveled in life.

I love Corey. I love him for what he is and what I am not. Innocence, untainted and yet not naïve, catches the essence of living through windows of the soul yet unsullied by life. Splendidly exuberant, he draws in all the energy of life, and expels it freely out to anyone who will embrace its gift. He is both a repository of living and the embodiment of simplicity. One without the other would dramatically diminish him, as it would any of us.

"I have 70 cents," he said. Sitting at a red light, I had no idea as to the nature, purpose or rationale of his comments. They arose, it seemed, from the incessant babbling and spontaneity that frequently marked him. "Dad, I have 70 cents."

Attending to the blur and bustle of the marauding traffic that rushed around me, I attempted to placate him, hoping that he would drift on to something else. "That's nice," I replied.

He was irritably insistent. My verbal pablum was blatantly insufficient. "Dad, I have 70 cents!" His voice was emphatic. I glanced in my rearview mirror and watched him squirming in his car seat, obviously possessing some agenda of great importance to him that was swallowed up in the supposedly greater agendas that dictated my day. Catching my eyes in the mirror, he held out a clenched fist. Clutching the coins and with dogged determination, he said, "Dad, I have 70 cents!"

What We Miss

I am occupied, attending to the congestion and myriad events around me. The traffic of my life is made up of frustrating red lights, a rare green one, and irritating yellows that flash across a myriad of my intersections. All of the congestion of commerce and career, the snarls of success and the raucous rhythm of rush hour: I embrace it all as essential and necessary to achievement. I am caught in the blindness of believing that living life means winning, being horrified that an opportunity missed is an unredeemable loss that creates a permanent setback and lifetime diminishment. I must master life by gorging myself on its complexities at every opportunity, without having time to savor the tender exquisiteness of its intricacies. Mine is a hoarding of life, rather than a delicate sampling. In and through it all, I miss the minute details in the mayhem, the subtleties that are the very essence of the larger things I feed upon. In essence, I miss simplicity. "I have 70 cents Dad!" It was a statement of simplicity, and so I missed it.

He had crystal blue eyes and romping blonde hair; his small hands cradled two quarters and two precarious dimes. They were clenched so firmly his tiny fingers turned shades of red and white. He held them valiantly in front of him with arms outstretched. His face was chiseled with a squared hint of boyish determination, the manifestation of four-year-old eyes, apprehending the core of life and living when I could not see it. He perceived with a clear soul what really mattered, when all I saw was an annoying red light and thick traffic. "Dad, I have 70 cents!"

And then I saw it. Quite by accident, it caught the barest edge of my mind. Out of the corner of my eye, from the furthest fringes of my life, it stirred. The simple intruded upon my chosen world of complexities. A solitary figure sat on the margins of my wild world, passing by me except for a four-year-old attuned to the wonder of simplicity, hoping that the din surrounding me might ebb just enough to catch a glimpse. I saw it. Scrawled by an unsteady hand across a tattered piece of discarded cardboard, stained and bent, were a handful of words. The edges of the cardboard were torn, frayed and mutilated, much like the man who held it. Primitive letters etched out the silent plea of a lost life. He was no more than 10 feet away, and I missed him. The sign read, "Need help, please."

"Dad, I have 70 cents!"

Simplicity Missed and Reclaimed

"Don't push these children away." The voice was purposeful, highlighting an eternal principle violated by stumbling men who chased after life and missed what it meant to live. "Don't ever get between them and me. These children are at the very center of life in the kingdom" (Mark 10:14 *The Message*). Simplicity is central to the infinite, which is an odd and incomprehensible dichotomy. That which is complex beyond comprehension embraces simplicity at its core and derives all that it is from that place.

Simplicity is the key that turns the tumblers to the door of the eternal. It is the single and sole passport to an audience with the infinite. We must suspect then that such a concept is built into the fabric of the finite as well. Simplicity is the essence of life and living from which all else springs. Without it, complexity loses it roots; it has no grounding, no boundaries and no identifiable point of departure that define and shape it. And it is here, with the cluster of children swirling around Him in innocent admiration, that Jesus declares simplicity as simply central.

The Pharisees and their malicious attempts to trap Him were barely hours old, still resonating in His mind. God incarnate, the Creator of the universe, was asked to justify Himself. It was indeed the absurdity that arises when simplicity is missed. The rich young ruler and the stench of materialism were only moments away. Face to face with God, he would prove himself unable to see Jesus in the tangled web woven of wealth and the complexity inherent in the sordid accumulation of power. He had too much of this world and too little of the next: all of which leaves no room for simplicity. The walk to Jerusalem; betrayal; spikes; a splintered beam; oozing blood; death — all of that was only days away. Awash in the many manifestations of man's sin and on the threshold of abolishing it, "Jesus gathered the children in His arms, and He laid His hands of blessing on them." (See Mark 10:16 in *The Message*.)

Simplicity Lived

As you look at this picture of Jesus, do you see it? It too is on the margins of

171

our lives, sadly so. He was sitting, gingerly drawing an armful of giggling and squealing children into His lap. The thick hands of a carpenter ran calloused fingers through mounds of curls gracing a tiny head, drawing a smile out of a timid child with a playful and slightly bemused stare. He embraced their innocence and simplicity as so far removed from the world He faced — the world He would die for. He saw, in their impish and innocent faces, the simplicity that keeps the world from seeing Him. He was at the vortex of His earthly life. In a matter of days, all of history would be rocked by His death. The universe would itself reel. Hell would fall. Satan would flee. The immensity of the powers of darkness would suffer complete and uncompromised defeat. He would defiantly tread the bowels of hell itself, and then He would rise. In His resurrection, He changed the entire course of human history for all time.

But there, at that moment, sandwiched between those cataclysmic events, He laughed with children who had no sense of who He was or what awaited Him. They were innocent. And so He played for a moment. He tickled and got tickled. He told a joke, and the air was filled with the squeal of childhood laughter. Eye to eye, with gentle intensity, He told them of their immense value and of a Father's love for each of them. He would die for them shortly, their innocence, perhaps, making that sacrifice more bearable and more compelling.

It was the Creator connecting through simplicity with the created, entirely unabated and unobstructed. It was the treasure of the deep soul finding connection with the vast God through the conduit of simplicity. The mayhem of life's traffic, all the red, green and yellow lights that had dogged His ministry, were laid aside so He could immerse Himself in life's real purpose.

The Door of Access
From this adoring pile of romping children, His gaze shifted, directing his words to the Twelve standing about. It was not to be a lesson for children, but one from them. Tussling with their youthful energy, He said, "Unless you accept God's kingdom in the simplicity of a child, you'll never get in" (Mark 10:15 The Message). The contrast was numbing, even paralyzing. The key to complexity was simplicity? But how could simplicity ever hope to grasp complexity? Simplicity would suggest intentional ignorance through the abandonment of the acquisition of knowledge. It was a

stunning reversal.

The complexities of life and living; the minute intricacies of the Law and the sacrificial system; the unfathomable breadth of the cosmos and starry hosts that begs exploration and contemplation; the mysterious, yet striking predictability of nature; the grandeur and the magnificent majesty of God; the incomprehensible I AM, next to which all of creation fades and pales into oblivion. Yet, all of this is accessed through simplicity? There, in the laughter and play of those children, lies the key to kingdom access and the sole passport to the infinite? It is too simple, so simple that grasping it is in itself complex.

Peals of laughter drew them back from contemplation, being a sweet elixir to a sullen life. They were the voices of those who had seized the keys to the kingdom through simplicity. It meant accepting as these children accepted, with innocence and simplicity, humility and obedience, through trust that never asks if there is anything else other than trust. These little ones engaged in a raw embracing, a simple acceptance free of attempts to determine how to shape one's life so that it might find a shred of acceptability before God. They accepted the unconditional as just that — unconditional. And so it was with these precious children.

Jesus stood, the lesson having been taught. He stooped, placed His hands on the children for a brief final moment and blessed them, extending into their simplicity the blessing of God. He was able to do so because of the space created in and by their simplicity. Access to the kingdom was granted, its evidence seen in the blessing. It is all so simple, yet so magnificently transforming. Many have expended lifetimes trying to achieve what these children achieved in but a moment via the vehicle of innocence and simplicity.

A final hug, a parting embrace and the children dispersed, running into the arms of waiting parents. A pair of them skipped off holding hands. Sticks trailed curlicue designs in the gritty dirt. Several ran around parents in errant circles of delight and innocent mischief. A small cluster gathered mounds of wildflowers, pressing their petals deep into their faces, inhaling their perfumed ecstasy. The sound of laughter faded and then dissipated on the soft winds of the day. The bevy of children scurried off to the next adventure, not realizing they had just had the greatest adventure of all. But simplicity embraced all of life as an adventure.

Getting Back
A honking horn exploded into the moment. The light was green. I instinctively punched the accelerator and drove off. "But Dad, I have 70 cents!" How our hearts are drawn to simplicity, yet how difficult it is for us to allow it to remain so; how painful it is when we cannot respond to it. Life caused me to drive by him, and to this day, I am irritated by that action. Corey and I talked about that man, and we talked about how we could help someone with his 70 cents: 70 cents of simplicity. Could I please have 70 cents of simplicity? I need just enough to see my world like Corey does. Oh God, could you please grant me 70 cents of simplicity?

How Do I Find 70 Cents of Simplicity?
How do I balance complexity with simplicity? How do I rectify the God of the universe playing with children and incorporate that principle into my world? How do I correlate the melding of the infinite and simplicity? Where is that common ground where I can embrace simplicity with a relentless vigor and yet live in a world of complexity?

It is not the absence of complexity, for creation is woven of it and it is the embodiment of God Himself. It is the example of the infinitely complex God playing and romping with simple children that we must seize, hold fast to and draw from. The key is the full embodiment of both simplicity and complexity, where neither is lost or sacrificed at the expense of the other, but where the complete embrace of both brings fullness and balance to life. The challenge is to hold to both equally. We assume that complexity is the absence of simplicity. Rather, is complexity not the very thing that highlights simplicity and makes it so very obvious and so deeply cherished? Is it not in the holding of simplicity that complexity has a point of origin and a benchmark that dictates its shape, tenor and tone? And is not the fullest embrace of the two, with each holding the other in balance, the very thing that maximizes life and living?

We need to live with 70 cents of simplicity, clutching it in our fists and refusing to let it go. We must allow it to hold and ground our exploration, acquisition and understanding of life's complexities. It is our task to apprehend an understanding of the world God has put us in, but, likewise, to maintain eyes of simplicity that keep us centered on that which is central to all of life. Complexity that is not continually grounded in simplicity is apt to be errant, causing us to be consumed in the complexity itself. For that brief moment, following a confrontation with the Pharisees, a pending confrontation with a rich young ruler, and only days away from death, Jesus centered Himself in simplicity. So should we.

Pondering Point
"I came so they can have real and eternal life, more and better life than they ever dreamed of" (John 10:10 The Message). Could it be that this "more and better life" is, in part, the ability to embrace complexity while holding tenaciously to simplicity, allowing simplicity to ground and center us in the complicated and detailed facets of life? Each provides a balancing effect for the other, thereby, allowing us to embrace the fullness of life without sacrificing anything that a single focus would cause us to miss. And is such a balance the work of God in our lives, His grace and power allowing us to achieve this dual embrace? Indeed, I think it is.

A Thought
- Which have I embraced: simplicity or complexity?
- How diminished is my life in the imbalance?
- How can I seek God in childlike simplicity this day?

Chapter 20

Pine Trees and Slips of Paper

Seventy years — as near as we could figure. They had silently stood guard, planted by people long dead several years before I was born. Standing as proud sentinels, for seven long decades, they had flanked the weathered cement steps that ascended our massive front porch.

These proud evergreens had faithfully stood by through the seasons, recording the process of our growing. They stood through summer's thick, sultry humidity, as my brothers and I sat on the wide porch swing, gliding deep into the temperate nights. In the autumn, they would watch as the three of us raked mounds of brightly colored leaves from around them, only to scatter them in wild and frenzied leaf fights. They waited in winter's chill until we would trudge down the long cement sidewalk and laboriously move drifts of windswept snow from the cement steps that were their charge. In the spring, they gracefully lifted their bows as, under my mother's careful supervision, my brothers and I planted clusters of geraniums and brilliant marigolds under their canopies before scurrying off to play with our friends. Inevitably, they came full circle, heralding summer's first days by tolerating three mischievous boys errantly rummaging through their foliage looking for bugs to add to their glass jar collections.

Childhood vanished. Time, unabated, rolled on. 1993 arrived all too quickly, finding me 12 years removed from the day I had left home and moved away from the two, faithful evergreens. Those 12 years had handed me three college degrees, a beautiful wife, and a bright-eyed daughter.

I returned home. Time had marked its advance, leaving deep footprints, a cruel reminder that we are on this side of eternity. The two evergreen sentries were marked deeply by the footprints of time. Watching those three boys for that many years had exhausted them. Our departure into adulthood, it seemed, had diminished them. They stood diseased and dying beyond redemption, holding our precious history in boughs now slumped and brown. There was no alternative.

With chainsaws in hand, we approached the two faithful trees. Standing before them, I wished they could speak. They would tell of events to which they had borne witness. I longed for a few final moments where, together, we could free our memories to run and leap and laugh in recounting many of the marvelous moments held deep in their branches. It was not to be. The chainsaws roared to life. With famished teeth, they gorged themselves on the heartwood of one, and then the other. In a matter of moments, both were helplessly prone on the ground, dead. Part of me was dead, too.

Then a thin slip of paper, caught in the swirling breeze produced from the falling boughs, was blown in a spiraling arc. Landing softly on the ground, it was a message from the past. I do not know how it stayed in the tree so long. It was not possible. Yet, it was dated April 18, 1971. Miraculously, for some 22 years, it had remained lodged deep in the branches. Faded and mottled by two decades of rain and snow and sun, it was a check, but it was so much more. Faded pen strokes, barely legible gave a hint to its origins. Squinting, I could still read the amount and the name. It was made out for the grand sum of $1.25, the cost of a week's worth of newspapers. The name inscribed on it — mine. Incredibly, it was a check written to me from one of my customers on my old paper route. Somehow I had lost it over two decades earlier. And somehow, someway, the evergreen had held it for me.

Holding this brittle and weathered check in my hands, the raw smell of the chainsaw exhaust still thick in the air around me, I was instantly transported back to a warm, wonderful time in my life. My old paper route. The faces of many of my old customers rolled warmly and easily through my head.

Old Mr. Hock with his cigar and bathrobe greeting me at his door every

Saturday morning. More often than not, the cigar was unlit. Mrs. Ryan always giving me hefty bags of fruit and mints at Christmas. Mrs. Tilly, older than old, counting out her pennies on her worn Formica kitchen table, making certain that she'd count out 50 for a tip. Mrs. Bland with her bleached hair and tight clothes in an attempt to halt the aging that had obviously already overtaken her. She always tipped, too. The Sawyer's – I always hoped that one of the daughters would come to the door; I was a boy after all. And the Clark's with six Siamese cats. You never knew if they wanted to love you or mutilate you. Across the street there lived Mrs. Warren with six romping Pomeranians. I thought it would be great to put those six cats and six dogs in an enclosed space and see what happened. I'd have wagered on the cats. My sturdy, ever-faithful Western Flyer bicycle with its three massive baskets. The two of us were indeed an awesome team, covering literally hundreds of miles and delivering thousands of newspapers together during those five, wonderful years.

Life from Death

"Lazarus, come out!" (John 11:43 NIV) The action was both implausible and incomprehensible. Mary and Martha had likely found the whole event uncomfortable, fearing it would terminate in the gross embarrassment and abject humiliation of their friend Jesus. "I know he will rise again in the resurrection at the last day" (John 11:24 NIV). Any thought of resurrection for them was likely connected to something far different than what was about to transpire. Their conceptualization of God was about to be shattered by His reality.

Loosely knit flocks of sparrows flitted in bobbing arches across a sky mottled with frothy clouds. Their spirited chirping set the cadence to their anxious flight. The sun threw thick shadows that were embossed by the torrential golden sunlight raining roundabout them. Tall grasses waved in gentle waltzes with a soft breeze, fully satisfied with the simplicity of a simple existence. Bees droned in lumbering arches, weighted with the bounty of the sea of wildflowers that lay strewn across the grassy landscape. Hills of content meandered out to the edges of the horizon, washed in ever thin hues of blue until they rolled off the horizon's precipice. Life was lavishly spread in abundance across warm meadows.

It was not life, but death that pressed weary feet shod in leather sandals cracked by long roads trod in hurried steps both panicked and pensive. A motley group of weathered messengers arrived exhausted and out of breath. Parched, hungry and layered in the dust of a hasty journey, they shook the accumulated filth out of weary robes. Eyes bloodshot and framed red by the collective wear of sun and gritty windblown sands drew themselves up from the dusty folds of faded robes and scanned the group for the object of their journey. His predominance was obvious. Something about Him lent an indescribable air of a bit of something all of us were intended to be; that calls to us from somewhere, but is, at the same time, far greater than any of us. Lips, chapped and dry, drew a touch of moisture into a parched mouth and said, "Lord, the one you love is sick" (John 11:3 NIV). The message was delivered in breathless urgency. Their eyes searched those of Jesus, hoping to draw from them the compassion and urgency that would stave off death.

Jesus paused and then placed a broad hand on the exhausted messenger. Squinting with an intensity that would accentuate His words and drive them deep into a frightened soul, He said, "This sickness will not end in death. No, it is for God's glory so that God's Son may be glorified through it" (John 11:4 NIV). Tears of relief edged burning eyes, then collected in tiny pools at their corners and traced rivulets of glistening release down cheeks burnt deep red by the wind and sun of a panicked journey. They wiped damp faces with the weary sleeves of worn robes, the fatigue of the journey somehow dissipated, the answer having re-energized the messengers with a mix of relief and hope that drove any physical fatigue into full submission. Glancing at each other, they drew themselves into a state of excited composure; looked at Jesus with the anticipation of children expecting some wonderful event for which they could not contain themselves; and urged Jesus' immediate departure. But He waited — for two agonizing days.

Jesus' agenda and the cadence of His work was not based in or on the need to outdistance death, somehow fearing that, should death beat Him to His destination, that all would be lost. Such a posture would assume the superiority of death, that death must be outflanked. For, if death claims the prize first, death will have won. And in the winning, the victory would be utterly irrevocable. But death did not set the agenda this day – or any day. Jesus set the agenda.

The setting of such an agenda was incomprehensible to the messengers, leaving them stupefied, forcing them to live two excruciating days of razor sharp anxiety. Theirs was a comprehension of a race, that whoever reached Lazarus first would be the victor. It is likely they did not doubt Jesus' ability to turn back the frigid hands of death. Likely, they doubted His ability to take back a life from those hands once they had laid their claim. Death was an irrevocable finality from which nothing returned. For two days, they sat on the sidelines of a race they felt they must win, watching the adversary take to the track uncontested, rapidly closing in on the finish line without so much as a challenge from Jesus. The 48 hours were deluged with confusion, anxiety and frustration.

Absurdity
We can believe to a point, but absurdity is that point beyond which faith wanes and then fails. Absurdity is often nothing more than God minus faith. It is our inability to release the infinite to be the infinite. Conversely, it is the refusal of the infinite to abide by our finite structures so that we might be able to force some pattern upon God that we find predictable. We imagine the impossible and what it might be in a given situation. And then we assume that our perception of the impossible is indeed accurate. Having fabricated our idea, we then naturally assume that whatever we've conceptualized is obviously what God will do. But the very conceptualization of the impossible is, in and of itself limiting, rendering a finite space within which the infinite is supposed to function.

But eventually He set out, two long days later. The journey terminated in what the messengers had both suspected and dreaded. Lazarus had died. The news hit them with a force of both grief and anger that toppled them emotionally. Their feelings proved right; their concerns about the delay were validated. The error of this prophet was verified, and His poor judgment was confirmed. Shaking heads were weighed down by sorrow and anger over this prophet who did not heed the call of reason and, by being so negligent, let a friend die. Sometimes God needs to listen, recognizing that, at times, even He may miss the slightest piece of information that had somehow escaped His notice. Such were the feelings of the messengers and those who had awaited His arrival. He was too late, and circumstances lay beyond even Him.

But Jesus did not understand His own limits. "Take away the stone" (John 11:39 NIV) was His response. In our estimation, even God can take on too much, His need for restraint outdistancing His commonsense. We want to stop Him in order to save Him from the folly of the infinite having gone too far. "But Lord ... by this time there is a bad odor, for he has been there four days" (John 11:39 NIV).

Even the crowd was held captive by their own limitations. "Could not he who opened the eyes of the blind man have kept this man from dying?" (John 11:37 NIV) The presumption was that death had placed Lazarus beyond the reach of Jesus. There was assumed a threshold beyond which all was irretrievable. It was believed that Jesus could thwart the reaching of that threshold, but once crossed, it was even beyond His grasp. Death was that threshold. It was irretrievable finality.

I wonder if somewhere in the back of their minds that day, those thoughts voiced a plea for restraint. But the words were spoken. The intent of Jesus' actions was made public. There was no room to turn back. In the end, the man walked out alive – impossibly alive.

Slips of Paper
I felt my father's hand set on my shoulder. I snapped back across those two long decades and dropped into the present moment filled with chainsaw exhaust, sawdust and death. I held a precious bit of history, crinkled, faded and weathered stiff. The trees would of necessity be cut up and used for firewood. Despite my desire to once again pick bugs from their branches; to plant flowers under their boughs; and to climb their heights to view the ends of the earth, that was not to be. In the march of time, we are born, we live, and we die. So it was with the evergreen sentries.

The trees, however, gave me something that did not need to die. They gave me something not bound by their lives or restricted by the finiteness of their existence. They gave me memories. They handed me a living piece of myself, forgotten except for a tiny slip of paper. Weakened by their death, I found untold strength in their memories.

Pondering Point
Had the trees not come down, the legacy tucked away on the slip of paper deep in their branches would not have been mine. It was there all along, inherent in them all that time. But it was only released to me at their death. And so it is with loss and death in our lives. There is something greater,

a morsel of the eternal released to us to illustrate the God who is on a scandalous mission to unceasingly create. And what greater display and more magnificent exercise of creative power than to create in the midst of the very thing that seems to so completely destroy — death? God is the infinite genius, not only building life from life – that is too easy – but rather, crafting life out of the raw material of loss and death.

A Thought
- What has been released to me in a recent death?
- Do I look for life to spring out of death?
- Can I view death as actually birthing life?

Contacting The Author

Craig Lounsbrough, M.Div.
Licensed Professional Counselor

19284 Cottonwood Drive, Suite 202
Parker, Colorado
80138 U.S.A.

303-593-0575 phone
303-840-0902 fax

www.craiglpc.com

Printed in the United States
220834BV00004B/2/P

9 781926 625270